THE STATE OF
BLACK
AMERICA 2004

Published by the National Urban League

Editor
Lee A. Daniels

Managing Editor
Rose Jefferson-Frazier

Associate Editors
David Brown
Serena K. Mayeri

IMAGE PARTNERS
CUSTOM PUBLISHING

President and Creative Director
John Shearer

General Manager
Ellen Burke

Art Director
JoAnn Jimenez

Associate Art Director
Louise Landry

Cover illustration by
Gary Neill

Background photo on cover
Wisconsin Historical Society
Image 6987

Copyright© National Urban League, 2004
Library of Congress Catalog Number 77-647469
ISBN 0-914758-87-X
$29.95

TOLLESTON

Michael J. Critelli
Chairman

Marc H. Morial
President and Chief Executive Officer

Michele M. Moore
Senior Vice President
Communications and Marketing

Paul Wycisk
Senior Vice President
Finance and Operations

Annelle Lewis
Senior Vice President
Affiliate Development

NATIONAL URBAN LEAGUE
INSTITUTE FOR OPPORTUNITY AND EQUALITY

William E. Spriggs
Executive Director

Lisa Bland Malone
Chief of Staff

James R. Lanier
Senior Resident Scholar for Community Justice Programs

Kenya L. Covington
Resident Scholar

Suzanne M. Bergeron
Manager for Legislative Affairs

Sherry Newton Dillard
Manager, Education Policy

Cheryl Hill Lee
Research Analyst

NATIONAL URBAN LEAGUE BOARD OF TRUSTEES

Officers

CHAIRMAN
Michael J. Critelli

SENIOR VICE CHAIRMAN
Charles M. Collins

SECRETARY
Alma Arrington Brown

TREASURER
Willard W. Brittain

**PRESIDENT AND
CHIEF EXECUTIVE
OFFICER**
Marc H. Morial

Contents

THE OP-ED SECTION

With Thanks

The

National Urban League

gratefully acknowledges the financial support of

The William and Flora Hewlett Foundation

for their generous grant

towards the publication and distribution of

The State of Black America 2004.

"The William and Flora Hewlett Foundation makes grants to address
the most serious social and environmental problems facing society,
where risk capital, responsibly invested, may make a difference over
time. The Foundation places a high value on sustaining and improving
institutions that make positive contributions to society."

From The President's Desk

The State of Black America:
The Complexity of Black Progress

By Marc H. Morial

Equality.

The word represents the essence of the American Ideal, and of the vision that has fueled and nurtured African Americans on their epic quest of nearly four centuries to hew a place of comfort and opportunity out of what is their native land.

If one were to envision *equality* as a three-dimensional entity, say, a carved teak treasure chest, inside would be a kaleidoscope of images and words and phrases of the American Experience—among them, *Give me liberty or give me death! ... We hold these truths to be self-evident .... with liberty and justice for all ... Fourscore and seven years ago... I have a dream today!*—that conjure up notions both concrete and ineffable.

We at the National Urban League embrace all the visions that flow from the consideration of the meaning of the word equality. However, the striving for equality by African Americans continues to be shadowed by an unsteadiness that has always cloaked the progress blacks have made in an extraordinary complexity.

We consider it critically important to Black America to quantify and enumerate just how far African Americans have climbed on the Index of Equality since that moment two centuries ago when the white men who constructed the American government created an invidious concept of measurement—three-fifths of a person—to define the value of the enslaved Africans and African Americans who were doing more than their share to build the American nation.

The enumeration of the status of African Americans is one of two new features being unveiled in the 2004 issue of *The State of Black America* by the National Urban League that will become regular features of publication: the National Urban League Equality Index and the National Urban League Survey.

What our Equality Index has determined is that now, 216 years after the Constitution of the United States of America was voted into being, black Americans, once defined as *three-fifths* stand at less than three-quarters—0.73, to be exact—of where White America stands.

That statistic, drawn from plumbing the status of black Americans in the five areas of education, economics, health, social justice and civic engagement, measures the "equality gap," the progress yet to be made before one can declare that black Americans and white Americans live in a society in which race produces no negative accounting.

America has a long way to go before that day will be reached. That reality is set out in stark fashion by the statistics of the Equality Index: The mean income of black males and black females is $16,867, and $6,370 less, respectively, than that of white males and white females. The black unemployment rate is more than twice that of whites—meaning that the number of unemployed blacks would have to decrease by 751,000 in order for the two unemployment rates to match. Less than 50 percent of African Americans own homes, compared to more than 70 percent of white Americans. The"equality gaps" in health education, and social justice are equally astonishing, if not more so.

The iteration of the gaps continues, and not only in the Equality Index, but also in the National Urban League Survey, which found, among other things, that 62 percent of African Americans feel the country is moving in the wrong direction. The collection of provocative essays and, another new feature, op-ed articles we've gathered provide a powerful resonance to the data limned in the Equality Index and the Survey.

For example, Samuel L. Myers, Jr. in his essay on African Americans' economic fortunes during the boom and bust of the last decade, writes of the "harsh and unusually adverse impact" African Americans have endured during this period of recession and post-recession. The combination of historical and contemporary anti-black discrimination in such areas of economic activity as jobs, home ownership, and access to capital for business development has meant that blacks "were less prepared to weather the bad times of the recession and have had greater difficulty taking advantage of the recovery and its associated benefits." Myers shows in keen detail that the so-called Long Boom of the 1990s benefited Black America in significant ways—but because their economic foundation was so thin to begin with, "The lesson to be learned from the long period of expansion is that African Americans are still perched precariously between a significant narrowing of income gaps and a persistent inequality in wealth."

The work of Myers and our other authors illuminate the fundamental characteristic of the African-American Experience: The Complexity of Black Progress.

That is to say that "black progress" has always been a complex matter. It has never been unalloyed, and never as clear-cut in the long run as the contemporary heralding of the progress make it appear.

That one can say this about the post-Reconstruction period is obvious. From the end of the Civil War to the 1890s, black Americans—even absent their 40 Acres and a Mule!—demonstrated a zeal for achievement and for taking full advantage of their new American citizenship that was nothing short of astonishing. But their proving white-supremacist ideology wrong earned them White America's fierce enmity, and via the Supreme Court's decision in the *Plessy* case, the retraction of virtually all facets of their rights as American citizens. The *progress* blacks had made since Emancipation was in several areas nearly wiped out—arguably, the dynamic of black business formation has never recovered—and in every field the rate of progress was severely retarded. It was only when African Americans regained their full civil rights in the 1960s that the group energy which was so apparent in the late nineteenth century could again burst forth. In that regard, it was no mere point of rhetoric that Martin Luther King, Jr. declared in his *Dream Speech* that it was "obvious that America has defaulted on [the] promissory note" it owed Americans of color; or that Whitney M. Young, Jr., leader of the National Urban League during the 1960s, who spoke just before King, warned, "The hour

13

is late. The gap [in resources and opportunities between blacks and whites] is widening ..."

The alarms they sounded then, which have been repeated by many since, and are repeated again in this volume of *The State of Black America*, point to the ultimate purpose of the work here. It is to advance the conversation about equality in America and among Americans, a conversation that has been and continues to be the essence of the American Experience.

The National Urban League Equality Index

By The National Urban League
Institute for Opportunity and Equality
and Global Insight, Inc.

Due to a production miscue, the last sentence of the first paragraph ends in an error.

The proper figure is 0.73.

he National Urban League Equality Index

By The National Urban League
Institute for Opportunity and Equality
and Global Insight, Inc.

The Equality Index is used to compare the conditions between whites and blacks in America using multiple variables. Article I, Section 2 of the Constitution of the United States counted an African American as 3/5 of a person for purposes of taxation and state representation in Congress, an Index value of 0.60. How much progress has been made in the United States in the last 216 years? The 13th Amendment, ratified in 1865, corrected this injustice, but according to the Equality Index, Black America still only stands at 0.76.

Whites have been used as the control in this index, so an index number of less than one means that blacks are doing relatively worse than whites in that category. An index value of greater than one means that blacks are doing better than whites in that category.

The Equality Index is a compilation of five sub-indices, Health, Education, Economics, Social Justice, and Civic Engagement. Each of these subcomponents has an index value of its own. The sections below will summarize how each of the individual sub-indices was constructed, the data available, and the weights used. Global Insight Inc. (GII) attempted to use the most recent data available across these 5 indices to create the most current index value. Additionally, GII attempted to anticipate media criticism of our methodology and the data used primarily by employing weighting schemes to manage shortcomings in the data. Index weights are represented within the text as either a percentage of the sub-index "Life expectancy is weighted at 20 percent," or a shorthand percentage follows the description of the data—"Live births per 1000 women was given the greatest value (0.05) in the index. "In all cases, the percentage is referring to the percent of the sub index being discussed. When referring to the entire Equality Index itself, the text will directly mention this. "The Education sub-index comprises 25 percent of the Equality Index."

The weights are as follows:

Economics	30%
Health	25%
Education	25%
Social Justice	10%
Civic Engagement	10%

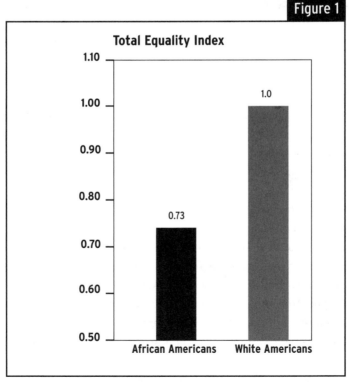

Figure 1

Total Equality Index

Note: This chart is comprised of a weighted index of the components represented in Figure 2.

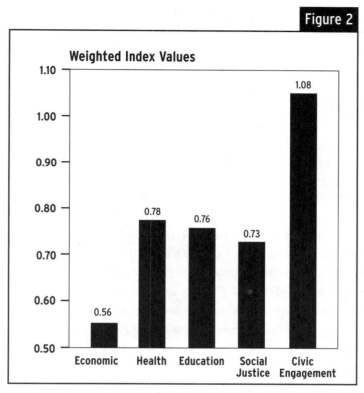

Figure 2

Weighted Index Values

Note: As in Figure 1 the index for African Americans as represented in this chart, is compared to a value of 1.0 for the white population.

Economics – 30% of the Equality Index

The Economics sub-index is divided into five separate categories: Mean Income, Employment Issues, Housing, Wealth Formation, and the Digital Divide. The weight of each category was based on relative importance and the quality of the data that was available. Of the six, Median Income was given the strongest weight (0.35), as it best indicates the relative economic performance of the black and white employed populations. Employment Issues was given a slightly lower weight (0.31), followed closely by Housing (0.30). Wealth Formation and the Digital

Divide were given only nominal weights. Wealth Formation was given a low priority (0.02); this category includes only a single data series. The Digital Divide was given a low weight of (0.01). Although this is an interesting area of study, it has only an ancillary impact on wages and standard of living. The overall index number for Economics was calculated at 0.56. As mentioned above, this translates into blacks performing disproportionately worse than whites in the economic criteria. A closer look at the sub-indices that make up the Economics index will reveal the reasons for the low index number.

Mean Income – 35%

The index for Median Income is broken out into three components: Mean Male Earnings by Highest Degree Earned (15 percent), Mean Female Earnings by Highest Degree Earned (15 percent), and Percent of Population Below the Poverty Line (5 percent). Mean Male Earnings produced an index value of 0.7. Not only are black males being paid less than whites, black males would have to see their mean income increase by $16,876 for the index to equal 1. The indicator for Mean Female Earnings of 0.83 reveals that black females are closer in earnings to their white counterparts. However, a black female would still have to earn $6,370 more for the index to reach 1.

Global Insight expects that over time, earnings between the two populations will converge, although they will not necessarily become equal. Data on the mean earnings by degree shows that blacks earn less than whites even when adjusted for education—this is in part due to degree choice. For example, education majors earn significantly less than business majors, a discrepancy which partly reflects the compensation for entering a less secure profession. In terms of risk versus reward, teachers and government workers are expected to earn less, as their jobs are largely immune to layoffs.

The Percent Below the Poverty Line category recorded a 0.33 index value. As a percentage of their population, three times as many blacks live below the poverty line as whites.

Employment Issues – 31%

Employment Issues is broken out into three categories. The Unemployment portion of the index was weighted at 29 percent, Labor Force Participation (LFP) at ages 16-24 was weighted at 0.5 percent, and LFP at age 25 and over at 1 percent. The Unemployment category itself is comprised of the overall unemployment rate (0.20), and also includes two categories for data on teenagers. The unemployment rate for blacks is more than twice their white counterparts, as is depicted in Figure 3, below. The number of unemployed blacks would have to decrease by 751,000 people for the Unemployment index to equal 1.

Figure 3

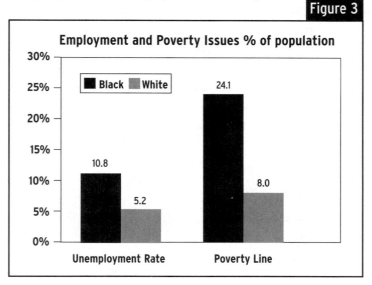

The Labor Force Participation (LFP) rate, on the other hand, showed a nominal racial difference. LFP is the number of people in a population that are either working or looking for work. The 0.97 index figure illustrates a slightly higher labor force participation rate for whites, and indicates a slightly higher number of discouraged black workers. If people feel that there is little probability of finding employment, there is a higher chance that they will drop out of the labor force. The slightly higher number of black people not in the labor force may be linked to a relatively high concentration of blacks in blue-collar positions. Historically, blue-collar jobs tend to see more attrition in times of economic hardship than white-collar jobs. In addition, the duration of a job search is higher for blue-collar jobs.

The LFP index number does not fully bring into perspective the difference in labor force participation, however. When this index is disaggregated by age and education level, the differences within are interesting. The LFP index for ages 16 to 19 was 0.68, but the LFP index for ages 20 to 24 showed improvement, at 0.88. The LFPs for higher age groups, simply stated as "over 25," are in addition broken out by education level. The LFP index number for Over 25 with Less than a High School Degree is 0.87.

However, the remaining LFP index values (all weighted at .001) all registered higher than one: High School Graduate/No College (1.08), Some College/No Degree (1.09), Associate's Degree (1.03), Less than Bachelor's Degree (1.07) and College Graduate (1.06). The numbers stress the importance of education. In particular, graduating from high school is a huge hurdle that can help to insure higher labor force participation for blacks. Higher education would not only insure higher LFP numbers but higher incomes as well.

Housing – 30%

The four Housing sub-indices are weighted according to their relative importance. Mortgage application denial was the most important (0.19), and weighted twice as strongly as the next item, Home Improvement Loans (0.09). The last two, Home Ownership (0.02) and Home Values (0.01), were given a very small importance in the index as those values are not current snapshots, but include historical material.

Home ownership, calculated at 0.63, shows yet another separation between races. Less than 50 percent of black families in America own homes. Conversely, over 70 percent of white families in the U.S. own homes. A contributing factor lies in the next series: mortgage denial was computed at 0.45. As a group, blacks experienced over twice as many mortgage denials as whites. Home improvement mortgage loans were slightly better than mortgage denials at 0.49. Still, blacks obtained home improvement financing at a rate that is half that of whites. Lower median income and other factors help to account for median home values, which was calculated at 0.65, translating into a $42,800 gap in black versus white home values.

Wealth Formation – 2%

There is also a huge disparity between the numbers of black- and white-owned businesses. The U.S. Firms by Race index, which was calculated at 0.37, illustrates the sizeable gap. There are nearly three times as many white-owned firms as black-owned firms in the U.S. (as compared to their relative percentages of the U.S. employment shares). The main reasons are that black firms either are not getting the seed money needed to create private wealth, and/or there is less entrepreneurial risk-taking in the black population. Both of these suppositions are supported in the Equality Index. Blacks are being rejected for home loans at a much higher rate than whites, and just as important, self-financing for blacks is far more difficult since the average black home is worth less than the average white home. The risk-taking argument can be supported by the higher numbers of blacks in jobs that have more security. Blacks are more likely to work in government and union jobs; both have greater job security than the average job. Of the two arguments, the index shows the greater influence is upon the first supposition, but possibly both theories are in operation.

The one caveat within this category is the elimination of 50/50 ownership and other firms. There were a large number of firms that reported ownership of the firm was 50/50 black/white, and there were many firms that responded "Other," meaning the people who owned it were either of mixed ancestry, or a race not covered in the survey response.

Digital Divide – 1%

Each of the two items within the Digital Divide category is equally weighted. There is pronounced disparity in racial access to computers and the Internet. The Computers at Home index number of 0.59 illustrates great difference between the percentages of black and white families that own computers. In addition, the Homes with Internet Access index produced a value of 0.51. Twice as many white families have Internet access as black families.

Health – 25% of the Equality Index

The Health sub-index is divided into three major categories: Death Rates and Life Expectancy, Lifetime Health Issues, and Neonatal Care and Related Issues. Of the three categories, Death Rates and Life Expectancy is the most important, so it has a weight of 45 percent within the Health Index. Lifetime Health Issues, which counts individuals who are impaired but still to some degree functioning, was given a weight of 30 percent. Lastly, Neonatal Care and early childhood issues were given a weight of 25 percent, since this stage of development sets the table for one's entire life, but is not always directly correlated to the health problems experienced later. The overall index number for Health was calculated at 0.78.

Death Rates and Life Expectancy – 45%

The white population in the U.S. lives longer than our nation's black population, and this large disadvantage is reflected in the Health Index. Life Expectancy at Birth is weighted at 15 percent of the index, and the Age-Adjusted Death Rate (per 100,000) for all causes is weighted at 30 percent. All causes were used in the index to avoid "cherry picking" any sub-causes that would skew the measurement in either direction. However, we will briefly note some of the more egregious examples that cause the black population to fall so significantly behind the white population in the Age-Adjusted Death Rate. Diabetes, homicide, and HIV prevalence in the black community are several times greater than in the white population. Diabetes is twice as likely to occur among blacks as whites. Blacks are five times more likely to die as the victim of a homicide. The disparity in HIV deaths is even more striking—blacks are almost 10 times as likely to have HIV compared to whites. A positive note for the black community is its dramatically lower rates of chronic lower respiratory diseases. In addition, the suicide rate of the nation's white population is twice that of blacks.

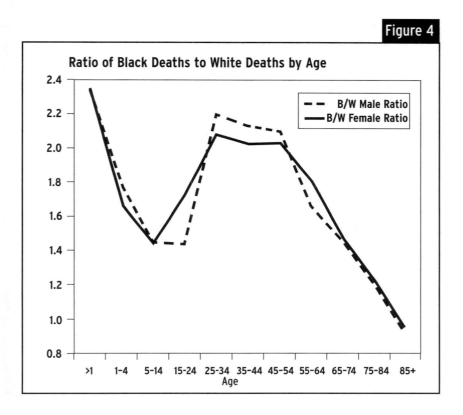

Figure 4

Figure 4 compares how many more times a black person is likely to die than a white at a given age. The category of Age-Adjusted Death Rates is based on two concepts; the first, discussed previously, lists risks due to individual disease and events. Figure 4 examines the differential using the second method, an age cohort pattern. Merely quoting the life expectancy differential—blacks live on average to age 72 versus age 78 for whites—does not adequately capture the lifecycle. What the average is masking is that blacks are dying in greater percentages than whites at every stage of life due to disease, accident, behavior, or as the victim of a crime. Note that in four age cohorts: Under 1 (>1), 25-34, 35-44, and 45-54, black males and black females are more than twice as likely to die than their white counterparts. Death rates for blacks compared to whites only start to converge after age 75.

Lifetime Health – 30%

This subcategory was further disaggregated into four sub-components. Weight Issues was valued at 15 percent, Substance Abuse 10 percent, Health Insurance 4 percent, and AIDS at 1 percent. Substance abuse and weight issues affect far greater percentages of the population than AIDS, and thus were given a greater importance in the index; furthermore deaths from HIV/AIDS were already counted in the previous category, so the effect of AIDS received a small weighting there.

Within the category of Substance Abuse, blacks fare on average better than whites. Greater usage of illegal drugs is cancelled out by less occurrence of heavy alcohol usage. Smoking is similar in both groups. Weight Issues, on the other hand, are lopsided. Blacks are more likely to be overweight, but even more likely than that to be obese. Within the index, obesity was weighted twice as heavily as merely overweight, since the health ramifications for being obese are far more significant. The third category, Health Insurance, measured the low propensity for African Americans to have health insurance coverage. Lower rates of health insurance are highly correlated with lower care, impacting health throughout a person's entire life. However, poor blacks were more likely to be covered than poor whites, making the top line disparity more likely to be caused by a lower rate of employer coverage. The final sub-component is AIDS. As previously mentioned, the black population has a much higher rate for AIDS, but the difference is even more dramatic for females. Black females are 20 times more likely to have AIDS than white females.

Neonatal Care, Mother's Health, Early Childhood – 25%

An improvement in the quality of care and preventative measures would go a long way in helping the black community achieve parity with whites in this portion of the sub-index. A higher average birthrate is highly correlated to less affluent societies, and it also results in the generational transfer of wealth being spread to more persons. Live births per 1000 women was given the greatest value (0.05) in the index. While the inability to conceive is a unique burden for every woman, it was assumed this challenge was roughly equal across populations and did not drive the higher birthrate differential. Maternal mortality (0.03) was the greatest differential in this data block. Simply stated, black women giving birth die at a far greater rate than white women, far more than can be explained by income alone. Substandard care, lack of access to care, lack of preventative medicine, and less education drive the gap in maternal mortality between blacks and whites. Black women giving birth are three times more likely to die than white women, a shocking statistic that should embarrass Americans and prompt immediate policy action. The remaining items in this category were all equally weighted at 0.03: Percent Live Births to Unmarried Mothers, Infant Mortality, Percent Births to Teenage Mothers, Uninsured Children, Children Covered by Medicaid, and Percent of Vaccinated Children in the First 3 Years.

Education – 25% of the Equality Index

The Education sub-index is divided into five major categories: Education Quality, Attainment, Scores, Enrollment, and Student Status . Of the five, quality is the most important, and thus it has a weight within the index of 45 percent. Within Education Quality are two sub-categories: Teacher Quality and Course Quality. Attainment (0.20) is considered almost as important, but the absence of both quality and degrees conferred gave it slightly less weight. Test scores are a good indication of how well a student is doing, but students considered in this data had not yet achieved the final goal of graduation, so a slightly lower weighting of 15 percent was assigned. Enrollment, which takes into account the benefits of education but obscures issues such as the "warehousing" of students, was given a weight of 10 percent. Lastly, Student Status and Risk Factors (0.10) were considered important measures of behavior, student confidence, and future accomplishment in life, but since these are closely related to attainment, a weighting of 10 percent was assigned. The overall index number for Education was calculated at 0.73.

Education Quality – 45%

The quality of the product being received within the black community and the white community is not equal. This fact dominates how each population fares in high schools, colleges, and their jobs across America. Two broad themes emerge from these criteria: the quality, skills, and experience of the teacher, and the course curriculum of the student. The first is referred to as Teacher Quality (0.30). This measure was consistently linked to student performance so was given the greatest weight. Four data series, each equally weighted at 7 percent, plus a fifth weighted at 3 percent, comprise this key determination. The first two, measure what percentage of teachers lack even a college minor in the subject they are teaching. The first series measures this factor at the middle-school level and the second at the high-school level. It does not measure what percentage of teachers achieved qualification certificates, only their prior college training in the subjects they now instruct.

Middle school showed the greatest black/white discrepancy—49 percent of teachers of black students did not have even a college minor in their subjects, compared to 40 percent for white students. Perhaps the most interesting linkage appears between this category and scores. The teacher quality indexes ratios are strikingly similar to the score ratios. Both hover in similar ranges, between 0.80 and 0.90. This seems to indicate black scores would improve if their teachers improved.

Two additional measures were used: Teachers with less than three years experience teaching in minority schools, and that "hidden teacher"—money. Funding was measured per student in high versus low poverty districts. Lastly, and only given half the weight of the prior four, is a California survey that asked what percentage of teachers in minority schools are under-prepared—that is, had not completed a California preparation program and obtained a full credential before beginning to teach. This variable was not given the full weight of the prior four, since California is only a subset of the nation.

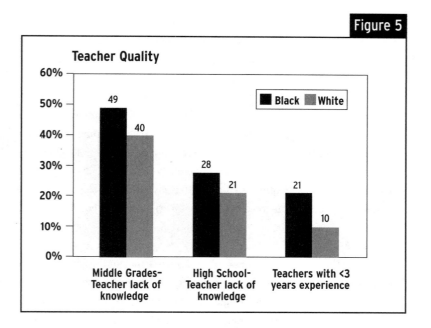

Figure 5

Attainment – 20%

To measure attainment, eight different gauges were used to create a range of "attained education." Each of these gauges was given an equal weight. Two of them measure graduation rates of two- and four-year schools; these are brand new data sets that actually tracked students over time. Unfortunately, this data is not yet suitable for release, and the official report has not been printed. However, the director of the study believes the preliminary numbers will be very close to the actual, and since our index uses a ratio of the two, these gauges were included. Additionally, NCAA Division I schools track how many of their college freshman graduate within six years. As it turned out, this ratio was exactly equal to the data from the study of enrolled students at four-year institutions, increasing our confidence in both measures.

The data shows that for current black graduation rates to equal white graduation rates at two-year schools, an additional 6,697 black students would have to earn an associates degree every year, an increase of 28 percent. To achieve parity at four-year schools, even greater efforts would be required. Another 23,698 black students would have to earn a bachelor's degree each year, an increase of 50 percent. Three data sets measured the degrees earned at the associate, bachelor, and masters levels. High school and college attainment for those over 25 were both also included in the index, as well as mean earnings by highest degree attained. For every ten whites that graduate with a college degree, there are just 6.3 blacks. Even if black students immediately begin graduating from college at a greater rate than whites, it would still take many years for the ratio of college degrees in the over-25 population to equilibrate.

Scores – 15%

In the category of test scores, nine different measures were selected (more were available) to create a range of "scored education." Each criterion was given an equal weight. Proficiency tests had the most data available, and included were reading, math, and science scores for both 9 and 17-year-old students. Additional ages and subjects were available, but they only diluted the impact of the core studies in the index. Both the ACT and the SAT were included, since they roughly cover different parts of the country, and their results did not significantly differ. Finally, very young children's test scores were included, as well as the evaluated skill sets (recognizing letters, counting to 20 or higher, writing their name, and reading or pretending to read) that children had when entering preschool. Interestingly, all 9 test scores showed little deviation between blacks and whites.

Enrollment – 10%

Eleven different measures were selected (more were available) to create a spectrum of "enrollment by age." Being enrolled in college during the more traditional age range of 18-24 was given far more importance than enrolling in college later in life. This was judged as appropriate because having a college degree at 20 rather than at 30 allows for the individual to earn higher wages for an additional 10 years.

Student Status and Risk Factors – 10%

Six evenly weighted items were included in this category. Dropping out of school is an important and widely followed statistic. Not only does it indicate students who have left the school system and thus don't "attain" the products of an education, it is also an indicator that the schools themselves are failing. The category Children in Poverty was included, since school performance is linked to conditions at home. Children with No Parent in the Labor Force was included for the same reason. Results of the next three items—Children with Disabilities, Suspended a Grade, and Repeating a Grade—illustrate the preponderance of black children to be quickly taken out of mainline classrooms.

Social Justice – 10% of the Equality Index

The Social Justice index, computed at 0.73, contains three categories: Equality Before the Law (0.80), Governmental Equality (0.15), and Victimization (0.10). The index number of 0.73 indicates unequal treatment received by blacks. Figure 6 illustrates some differences among the key variables.

Equality Before the Law – 80%

The first and most important category in the Social Justice sub-index is the equal treatment of blacks and whites before the law in our society. This is the essence of a fair and colorblind nation. Four data series captured this idea best: Stopped While Driving, Average Jail Sentence, Probation, and Prisoners as a Percent of Arrests.

Stopped While Driving (0.20) measures the percentage of drivers being pulled over for a variety of reasons. If we had simply used the total percentage, it would have produced an index of 0.85, since the average Stopped While Driving for blacks is nearly 2-percentage points higher than whites—12.3 percent versus 10.4 percent. However, not all cars being stopped are equal. Speeding, Vehicle Defects, and Roadside Checks for drunk drivers do not involve subjective thinking, therefore these three items were given only the total value of the Stopped While Driving index. Record Checks, Driver Suspected of Something, and "Other" were weighted far more heavily within Stopped While Driving. They comprise 75 percent of the index, because they are more subjective decisions. As expected, these weights caused the index value to decline—their results are less favorable to the black population. GII calculated that if using the simple total percentage figure, for the Stopped While Driving index to equalize at 1, the number of blacks stopped would have to shrink by 344,780 persons.

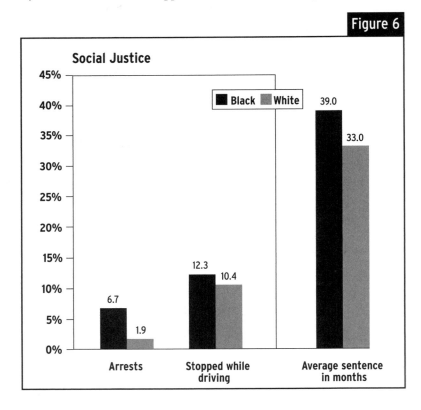

Figure 6

Social Justice

The index figure for Average Jail Sentence (0.20) shows that blacks are receiving, on average, a slightly longer felony sentence relative to whites. A black person's average sentence is six months longer than a white's. This index has a value of 0.85. Obviously, this series could be open to criticism, since not all felonies are equal crimes. Depending on the mix of crimes committed, this index may be lower than .85, or even higher than 1.

Of the sentences issued in 12 crime categories in the State Courts, black sentences were longer than white sentences in 11 of them. Only for murder did whites receive a longer sentence than blacks, which raises the question: Are whites more likely to receive longer lifetime sentences and blacks more likely to receive the death penalty? The data sets could not answer this question.

According to Probation (0.20) figures, white felons are more likely to get probation than black felons. This result produced a Probation Grant index of 0.83. Again, this data series was adjusted for what kind of crime placed the person in jail, so a non-violent criminal offender was granted probation more often than a violent offender. Not included in this index, but related to the percentage of those who get probation, is how long a felon remains on probation. On average, a white felon's probation is 36 months long, and black felon's is 37 months long. So not only are whites more likely to get probation, but they serve slightly shorter probation terms.

Prisoners as a Percentage of Arrests – 20%

This index measures the transition from arrest to prisoner, and the discrepancy therein. The index value of 0.32 speaks to the disproportionate amount of black arrests that result in the person becoming a prisoner. In fact, as a percentage of arrests, there are three times as many blacks that become prisoners. The operating theory is blacks are more likely to be imprisoned once arrested. Alternative theories would have to suppose that too many whites are being falsely arrested and then must be freed, or not enough blacks are being arrested based on their reported crimes.

Governmental Equality – 15%

This index was constructed to measure government treatment of blacks in two categories. The categories are evenly weighted at .075. State and Local Government Employment Median Pay, which produced a 0.85 figure, displays a discrepancy in pay between the races. Median Government pay for blacks would have to rise by $5,200 to equal whites. The next indicator relates to how many people are receiving Temporary

Assistance for Needy Families (TANF) as a percent of children living below the poverty line. The index value of 0.38 illustrates that white children living in poverty are three times as likely to be receiving TANF benefits than the average black child.

Victimization and Mental Anguish – 10%

The Homicide indices for males and females comprise half the index under this category, and the remainder is calculated by Adolescent Mortality (ages 13-19). Homicide rates, both male and female, paint a grim picture here. The Homicide Index number for males (0.025 weight) shows a murder rate for black males that is seven times that of white males. Under Male Homicides, black male deaths due to firearms and stabbings are near the overall index value of 0.15, but white males are more likely to die due to vehicular accidents. The Homicide index number for females was slightly better, but still only 0.28. The homicide rate for black females is over three times higher than white females. Lastly, the category of adolescent or teenage deaths from all causes had more black deaths than white for an index of 0.80.

Civic Engagement – 10% of the Equality Index

Civic Engagement sub-index is divided into four categories: The Democratic Process (0.50), Volunteerism (0.30), Collective Bargaining (0.10), and Government Employment (0.10). The Civic Engagement index number was computed at 1.08. This means that, as far as Civic Engagement goes, blacks in America are more involved than whites. Figure 7 at the end of the section graphically demonstrates some of the differences among variables.

The Democratic Process – 50%

This category attempts to measure the degree to which the two populations exercise their right to vote. Registering to vote and the act of voting itself are excellent proxies for how invested people are in the fabric of their nation and to what extent they feel engaged in their society. Citizens generally don't vote when they express little interest in their representatives, or when the issues being decided aren't perceived to be of consequence to their daily life. Registered voters (25 percent) and actual voters (25 percent) are weighted evenly within this group. The Registered Voter index figure of 0.97 speaks to a slightly higher percentage of whites registered to vote than blacks. The number of black registered voters needs to rise by 482,000 people for the Registered Voter index to reach 1. The Actual Voter index value of 0.95 also shows a nominal difference between blacks and whites. Interestingly, despite the tremendous effort it took to gain the right to vote, blacks participate somewhat less than whites.

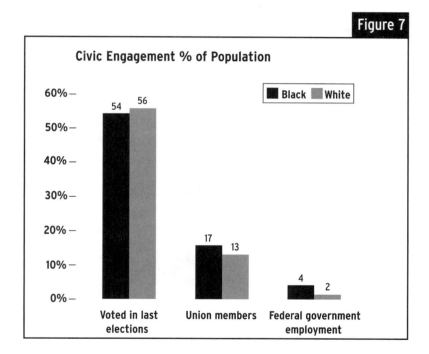

Figure 7

Civic Engagement % of Population

■ Black ■ White

Voted in last elections: Black 54, White 56
Union members: Black 17, White 13
Federal government employment: Black 4, White 2

Volunteerism – 30%

Volunteering has two components: Community Volunteerism (20 percent) has twice the importance as does Military Volunteerism (10 percent). The Community Volunteerism figure is 0.79, meaning a higher percentage of whites opt to volunteer at home, but the index figure for

Military Volunteerism is 1.45, indicating a substantially higher percentage of blacks volunteer in the military reserves. Part of this may be due to income supplementation, which is why military volunteerism is not pure "volunteering" and thus given a smaller weight.

Collective Bargaining – 10%

The two components of this category, Unionism (% in unions) and Union Represented (% in occupations that represented by Unions) are equally weighted. The Unionism index number of 1.3 reveals a significantly higher percentage of blacks in unions than whites. In addition, the Union Representation index value of 1.3 means that blacks also are more concentrated in jobs that are represented by unions.

Governmental Employment – 10%

There are also two components in this category: State and Local Government Employment and Federal Government Employment. They are evenly weighted. The Federal Government Employment index tallies at 1.95, demonstrating a great difference between white and black government employment at the federal level. The State and Local Government index was calculated at 1.35. The large index numbers may speak to the security that comes along with government employment. In addition, government jobs tend to have good health benefits, which may be another attractive feature.

he National Urban League Survey

By Dr. Silas Lee

Methodology

The National Urban League initiated the 2004 baseline poll to develop a benchmark for measuring the comparative attitudes of African Americans, Hispanic Americans and Asian Americans toward the quality of life in their communities, and pertinent social, economic and political issues.

Between January 28 and February 10 700 African-American and 200 Hispanic-American and 200 Asian-American adult respondents respectively were interviewed by a professional interviewing service. The respondents were selected from a random digit dial database to ensure a representative sample of the demographics of the respective ethnic groups.

The poll has a Margin of Error of + or –4 percent. For the smaller sub-sample of Hispanic and Asian Americans, the Margin of Error is slightly higher.

1. GENERAL LEVEL OF SATISFACTION

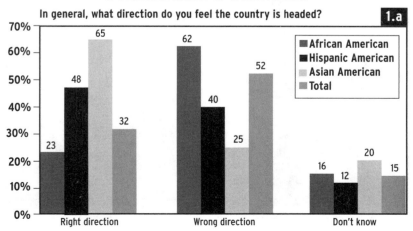

In general, what direction do you feel the country is headed? 1.a

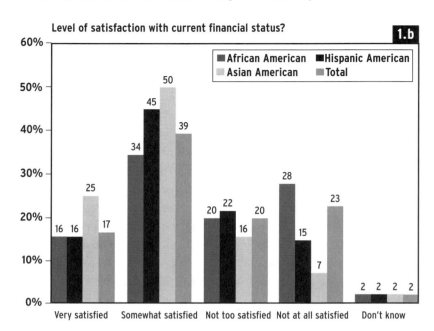

Level of satisfaction with current financial status? 1.b

Legend: African American, Hispanic American, Asian American, Total

- Very satisfied: 16, 16, 25, 17
- Somewhat satisfied: 34, 45, 50, 39
- Not too satisfied: 20, 22, 16, 20
- Not at all satisfied: 28, 15, 7, 23
- Don't know: 2, 2, 2, 2

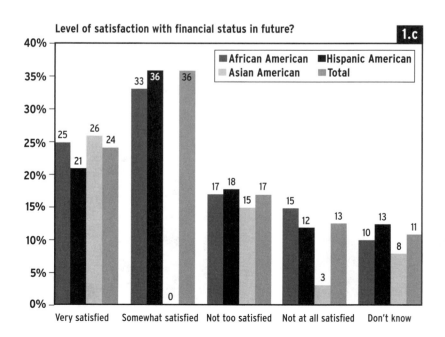

Level of satisfaction with financial status in future? 1.c

Legend: African American, Hispanic American, Asian American, Total

- Very satisfied: 25, 21, 26, 24
- Somewhat satisfied: 33, 36, 0, 36
- Not too satisfied: 17, 18, 15, 17
- Not at all satisfied: 15, 12, 3, 13
- Don't know: 10, 13, 8, 11

2. SINCE 1963

Which strategy will be most effective at solving the problems affecting African Americans, Hispanic Americans, and Asian Americans?

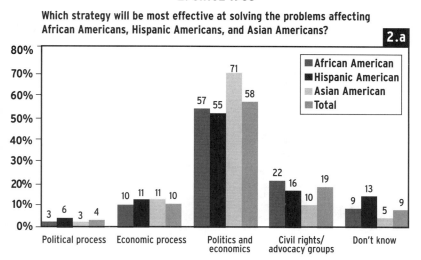

Degree of improvement in the quality of public education since the passage of the Civil Rights Act?

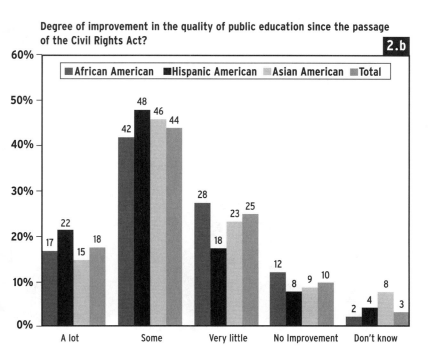

Degree of improvement in housing integration since the passage of
the Civil Rights Act?

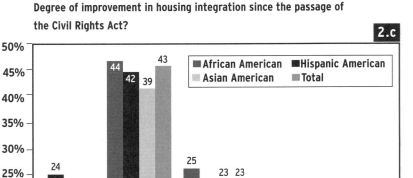

Degree of improvement in access to decent jobs since the passage of the
Civil Rights Act?

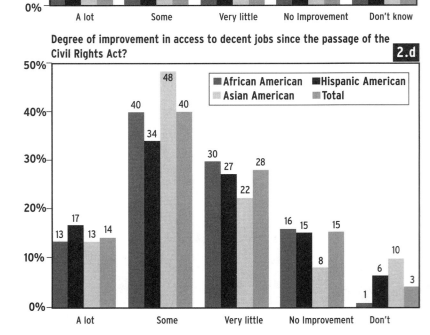

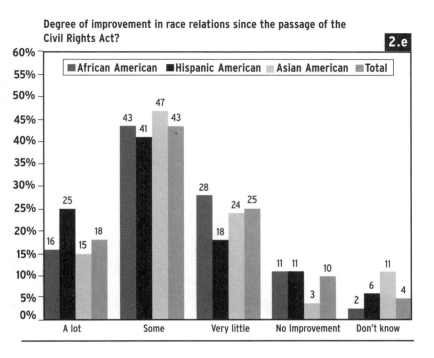

Degree of improvement in race relations since the passage of the Civil Rights Act?

2.e

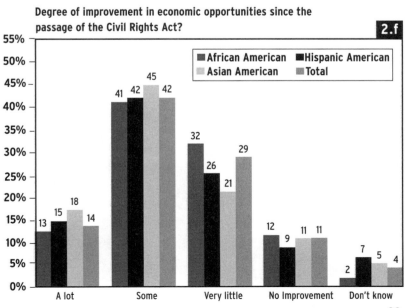

Degree of improvement in economic opportunities since the passage of the Civil Rights Act?

2.f

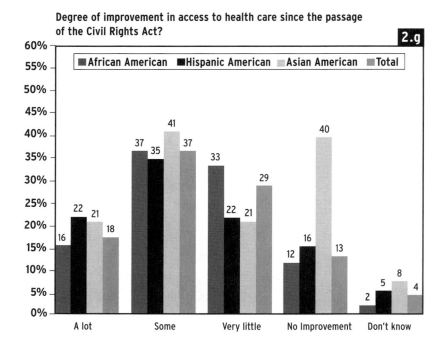

Degree of improvement in access to health care since the passage of the Civil Rights Act?

2.g

3. EMPLOYMENT/WORKPLACE

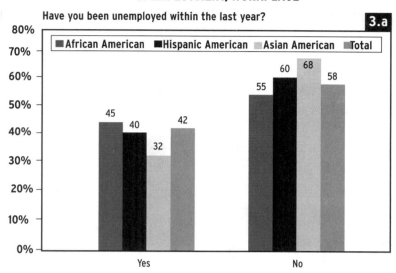

Have you been unemployed within the last year? **3.a**

■African American ■Hispanic American ▨Asian American ▨Total

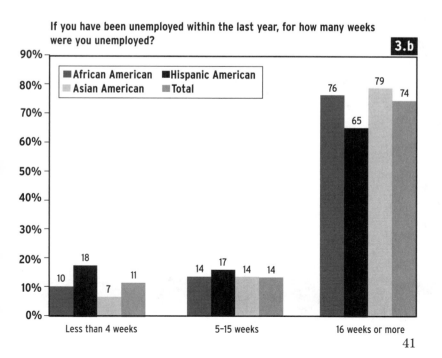

If you have been unemployed within the last year, for how many weeks were you unemployed? **3.b**

■African American ■Hispanic American ▨Asian American ▨Total

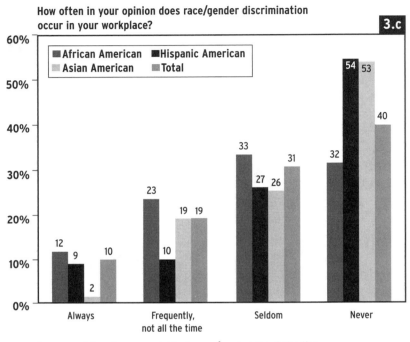

How often in your opinion does race/gender discrimination occur in your workplace?

3.c

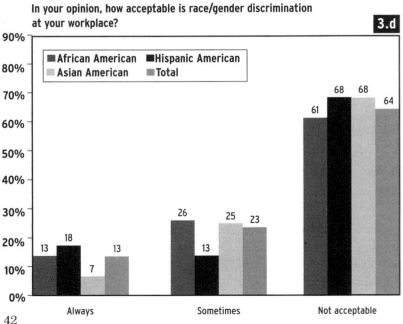

In your opinion, how acceptable is race/gender discrimination at your workplace?

3.d

4. UTILIZATION OF FINANCIAL SERVICES

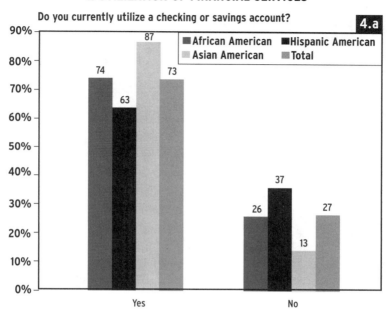

Do you currently utilize a checking or savings account?

4.a

- ■ African American
- ■ Hispanic American
- ■ Asian American
- ■ Total

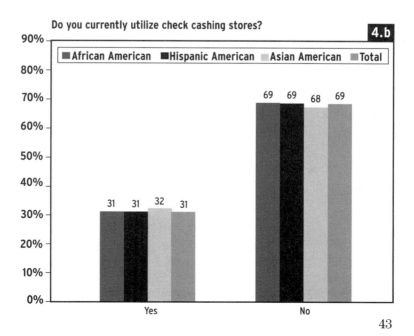

Do you currently utilize check cashing stores?

4.b

- ■ African American
- ■ Hispanic American
- ■ Asian American
- ■ Total

43

Do you currently invest in stocks, bonds, or a particular pension plan?

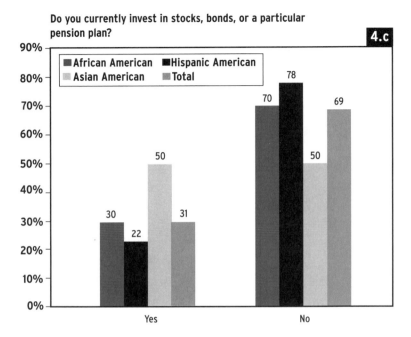

5. HOME OWNERSHIP

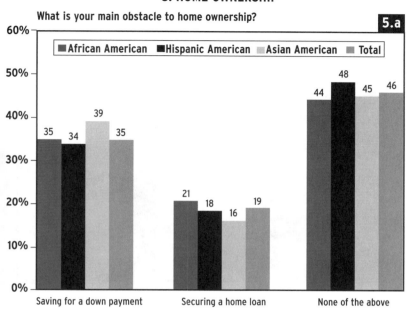

What is your main obstacle to home ownership?

5.a

6. HEALTH

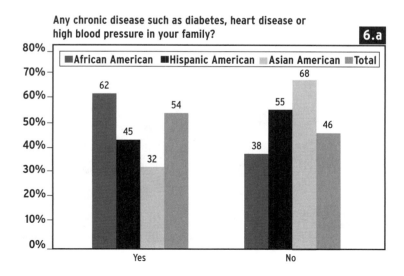

Any chronic disease such as diabetes, heart disease or high blood pressure in your family?

6.a

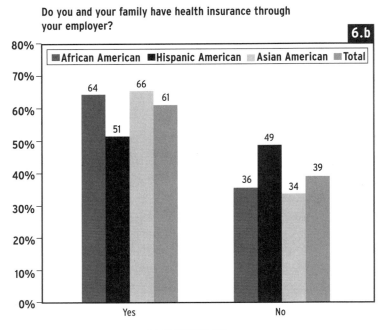

Do you and your family have health insurance through your employer?

6.b

7. EDUCATION

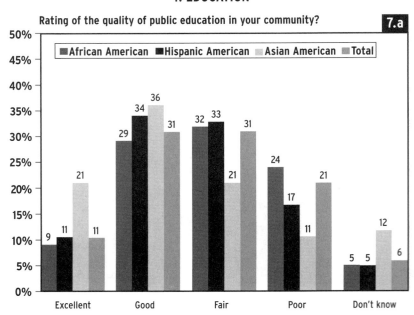

Rating of the quality of public education in your community?

7.a

Are public high school graduates adequately prepared for college/technical school or work force?

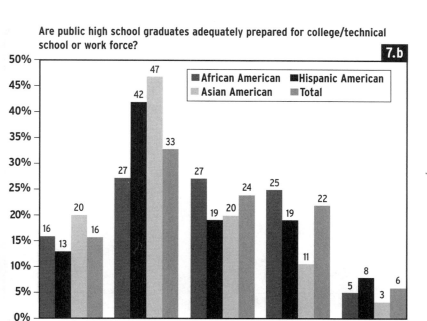

Importance of early childhood education?

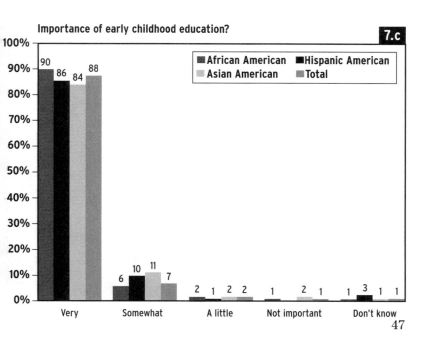

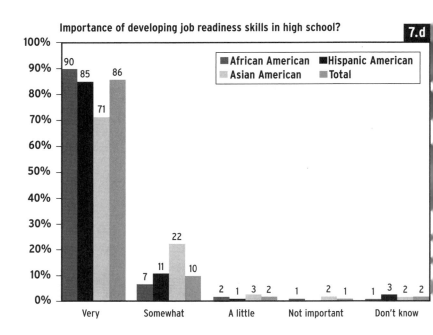

Importance of developing job readiness skills in high school? **7.d**

8. CRIMINAL JUSTICE

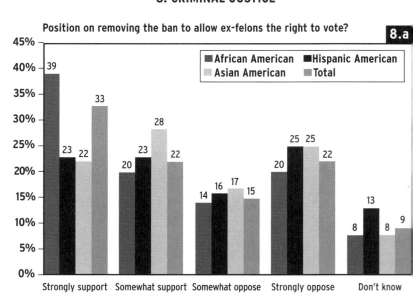

Position on removing the ban to allow ex-felons the right to vote? **8.a**

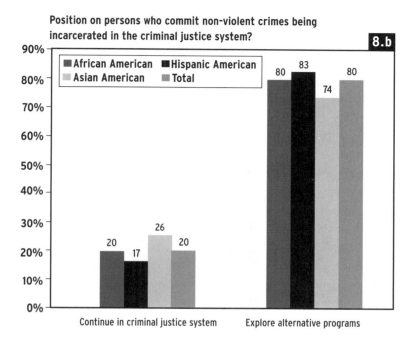

Position on persons who commit non-violent crimes being incarcerated in the criminal justice system?

8.b

Legend: ■ African American ■ Hispanic American ■ Asian American ■ Total

Continue in criminal justice system: African American 20, Hispanic American 17, Asian American 26, Total 20

Explore alternative programs: African American 80, Hispanic American 83, Asian American 74, Total 80

9. CIVIC ENGAGEMENT

Do you feel that elected officials are responsive to the needs of the constituents?

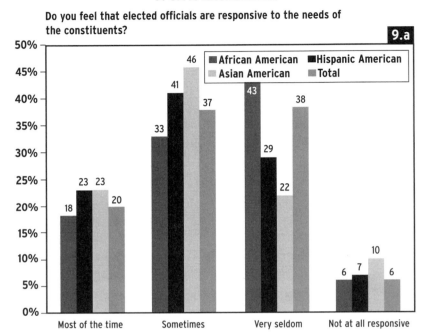

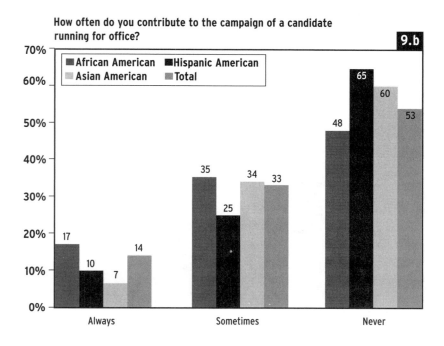

How often do you contribute to the campaign of a candidate running for office?

9.b

African-American Economic Well-Being During the Boom and Bust

By Samuel L. Myers, Jr.

Introduction

The period from 1990 to 2000 was one of the most sustained periods of prosperity of the 20th century. During this long period of economic growth, African-American household incomes soared and some measures of income and wage disparities between blacks and whites narrowed. Unemployment rates reached historic lows and the racial differential in unemployment declined. Indeed, during the last years of the boom, black unemployment rates reached their lowest levels since the collection of detailed racial statistics on unemployment began in the 1970s. There is no dispute over the fact that African Americans as a group benefited from the expanding economy.

The expansion reversed and by March 2001 the economy was officially in a recession. The events of September 11, 2001 and its aftermath of depressed economic activity in many industries have had a harsh and unusually adverse impact on African Americans. Even as the economy rebounds, it is too soon to know whether the temporary deterioration in the relative economic well-being of African-American households will retard a full recovery to the heightened level of economic prosperity that African Americans experienced in the 1990s. But, it is helpful to revisit the boom years and digest what did and did not happen during that period.

The main story we tell in this chapter is that during the boom years much of the improvement in relative economic well-being of African

Americans was concentrated in current income measures. By way of contrast, among African Americans, wealth measures did not see the same sustained surge nor was there a sizeable change in financial assets that would help African-American households weather an economic downturn. Residential mortgage credit, a key component of the wealth creation nexus, became more affordable at the very moment that fewer African-American households were able to take advantage of falling interest rates.

In short, the boom years reveal a major fault line in the nature of wealth acquisition within the black community. The bust years may be uncommonly painful because wealth inequalities persist.

The Boom and Bust

The 1990s were a decade of unprecedented prosperity. It was a period of one of the longest non-inflationary economic expansions in memory. Unemployment rates fell from 7.8 percent at the peak of the recession in June 1992 to 3.8 percent in April of 2000.[1] The number of employed persons soared from 118 million persons in January 1992 to nearly 138 million persons in January 2001. Mean family net worth (expressed in 2001 dollars) soared from $230.5 million in 1992 to $395.5 million in 2001.

Then recession struck. The world witnessed the horrific bombing of the World Trade Towers and the Pentagon, critical industries faced massive reductions in revenues, stock market prices plunged, and state and local governments once swamped with surpluses faced daunting budget deficits. In June 2003, the unemployment rate rose to 6.3 percent, and by January 2002 total employment fell to 135.7 million. At the time of this writing, in January 2004, when the economy officially is in a recovery, only 689,000 more workers are employed than in January 2001.

It is too soon to know how these major reversals of fortune will affect African-American communities in the long-term. Due to the lag in data availability, it is also often difficult to pinpoint the emergence of short-term impacts. Nevertheless, it is useful to review the pathways that led to the current situation, explore in some depth the period of prosperity of the 1990s, and offer an assessment of how African Americans fared during the last decade preceding the most recent downturn and ambiguous recovery.

Household Income Measures of Well Being

One measure of relative economic well-being is the ratio of black to white household incomes. The averages can be measured by means or medians. Means capture the idiosyncratic impacts of excessively high income households. Medians indicate the midpoint of all incomes; half of all households received less than the median while half received more than the median. The measure of household income includes wages and salaries, self-employment income, rents, royalties, and income earned on savings and investments. Figure 1 shows that there was an upward trend in both black-white median and black-white mean zhousehold incomes over the past decade.

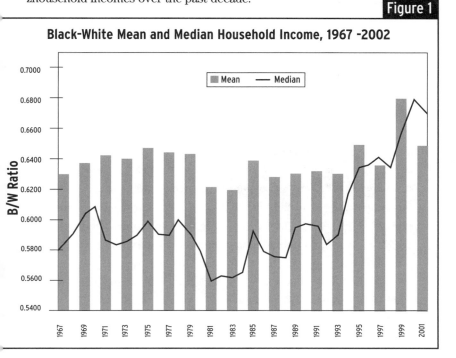

Figure 1

Black-White Mean and Median Household Income, 1967 -2002

The 1990s saw the longest sustained increase in the ratio of black to white median household incomes since 1967. Although there were other spurts of improvement (1972-1975, 1981-1985, 1988-1990), the uninterrupted growth in median black household income relative to median white household income from 1992 to 1997 is impressive not only by its longevity, but also by the heights it reached. In 1992, the ratio was .5823. It rose sharply to .6428 by 1997.[2]

The ratio of black to white mean household incomes also rose from .6269 in 1992 to .6625 in 1996. The graph shows a dip in both the black-white median and the black-white mean household income ratios in 1998, with additional declines in 2000 and 2001. Still, the decade-long period reveals an overall upward trend in both measures. The peak was reached at the end of the decade and was followed by a downward spiral as we entered the 21st century.

Individual Wage and Salary Incomes

The same progress is not quite as evident when comparing census figures on the most important component of household income: the wages and salaries of individuals. In 1990, the average wage and salary income reported for black males was $23,973.44 (in 2000 dollars). This rose to $27,449.63 in 2000. The average wage and salary income reported for white males in 1990 was $37,025.77. This rose to $42,779.90 by 2000. Thus for males, the black-white ratio of wage and salary incomes was about the same in 2000 as in 1990 (64.16 percent versus 64.75 percent). Meanwhile, the ratio of black to white wage and salary income for females fell from 94.85 percent based on 1990 wage and salary incomes of $18,919.46 and $19,945.95 to 91.17% in 2000 based on incomes of $22,577.56 and $24,764.12. Therefore, despite the dramatic growth in real black wage and salary incomes, the relative position of black males was stagnant and the relative position of black females deteriorated. Overall, the ratio of black to white wage and salary incomes fell slightly from 73.47 percent to 72.50 percent.

Others have claimed that the deteriorating position of black wage and salary earners is the result of retrenchment in manufacturing industries, where blacks earn good wages but also where jobs are disappearing (Boushey and Cherry 2003). To construct Figure 2, we have used the Current Population Survey March Supplement Series to illustrate the ratio of black to white wage and salary incomes for males and females, over 20 years of age, in manufacturing industries. The figure does not show a consistent downward trend throughout the period, but it does suggest the deterioration of black female incomes during the last recession.

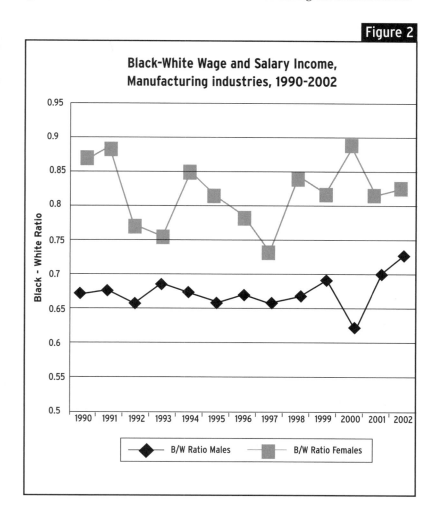

Figure 2

Black-White Wage and Salary Income, Manufacturing industries, 1990-2002

Wealth and Net Worth

Whereas income is a flow, wealth is a stock. Measured in real 2001 dollars, mean net worth exploded from $280,500 in 1992 to $395,500 in 2001.[3] The net worth of white, non-Hispanic families grew on average from $274,800 to $482,900. Average non-white wealth only increased from $95,800 to $115,500. The mean wealth of African-American families increased from $59,400 to $75,700 between 1992 and 2001.

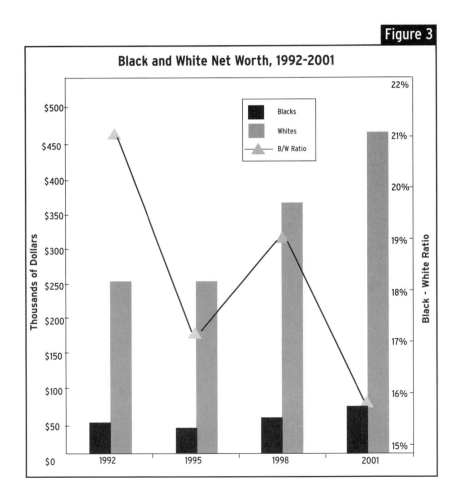

Figure 3

Black and White Net Worth, 1992-2001

Therefore, during this period, the wealth gap—far larger than the income gap—widened while the household income gap narrowed. Black net worth plunged from nearly 22 percent of white net worth in 1992 to barely 16 percent of white net worth in 2001. Or put differently, the white net worth was 4.6 times greater than black net worth in 1992.[4] By 2001, the gap widened such that white net worth was 6.2 times greater than black net worth. As Figure 3 graphically depicts, the boom years of the 1990s saw white wealth grow much faster than did black wealth. As a result, the racial gap in wealth widened substantially.

Moreover, there are troubling differences in the types of assets held. Of the $44.373 trillion in assets held by whites in 2001, 43 percent or $19.222 trillion were financial assets. Financial assets include stocks, bonds, and other liquid investments. Only 25.9 percent of white assets were held in their homes. Of the $1.493.3 trillion in assets held by blacks, 42 percent were held in their homes while only 33 percent were held in financial assets.[5] On the liability side, blacks held nearly five times more installment debt than whites and nearly three times more debt than whites overall.

Credit Markets and the Black-White Disparity

Fundamental changes in credit markets occurred during the 1990s. Mortgage lenders introduced new and improved instruments to speed the review and approval of loan applicants. Large secondary market participants like Freddie Mac and Fannie Mae developed tools to assist lenders in streamlining the application process and hopefully to reduce racial disparities in lending. By using more objective criteria to evaluate credit risk, the thinking went, these government-sponsored enterprises would help reverse a long-standing pattern of significant racial gaps in loan denials.

Moreover, the new millennium marshaled in a period of extraordinarily low interest rates. Investors could borrow and plow their funds into money-making financial instruments; homeowners could refinance and lower their debt. New homeowners could amass assets at a fraction of the cost that previous cohorts experienced.

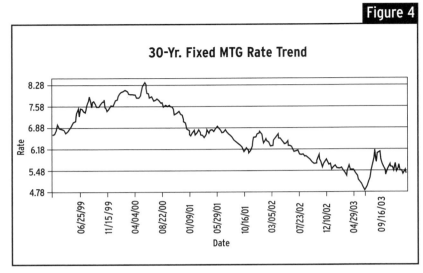

Figure 4

30-Yr. Fixed MTG Rate Trend

Source: http://www.bankrate.com/brm/graphs/main_graph.asp, accessed 01/10/04

The period that began in the second quarter of 2000 and continued well into Spring 2003 ushered in one of the most dramatic slides in home mortgage interest rates in history. Figure 4 shows that after peaking at about 8.28 percent in early 2000, 30-year fixed rate mortgage interest rates declined to less than five percent by May 2003. Thus, the decline in annual interest rates from 2000 to 2002, which is shown in Figure 5, was just the start of a steady decline that lasted for three years. During this three-year period, however, loan applications filed by African Americans for conventional home mortgages declined In 2000, African Americans filed 518,275 such loan applications but they only filed 371,386 conventional home purchase loan applications in 2002.[6] Black loan denial rates, which were more than 50 percent in 1997, fell to 44.5 percent in 2000 and declined further to 26.3 percent in 2002. But, white loan denial rates also fell during this highly competitive period where banks were literally giving loans away. As a result, the black-white ratio of loan denial rates rose from a low of 1.92 in 1999 to 2.27 in 2002.

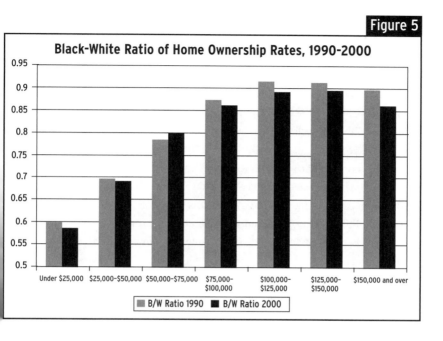

Figure 5

Black-White Ratio of Home Ownership Rates, 1990-2000

Legend: ■ B/W Ratio 1990 ■ B/W Ratio 2000

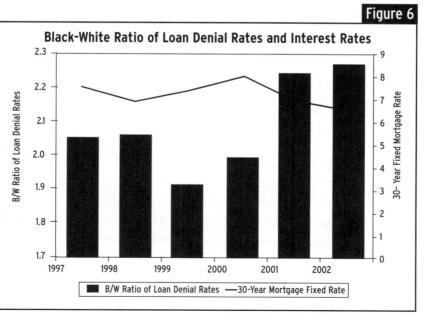

Figure 6

Black-White Ratio of Loan Denial Rates and Interest Rates

Legend: ■ B/W Ratio of Loan Denial Rates —30-Year Mortgage Fixed Rate

Despite the decline in loan applications, black loan originations—loans that are approved by the lender and accepted by the applicant—increased from 139,544 in 1997 to 189,817 in 2002.[7] Moreover, the aggregate value of these loans increased (in constant 2000 dollars) from $11.583 million to $25.244. During this period, the average approved loan amount jumped from $83,000 to $133,000. Figure 5 shows that these increases in the average amount of originated loans rose faster among blacks than among whites and helped narrow the still significant gap in home purchase loan amounts provided to African Americans versus those to whites.

The upshot of these changes in credit markets is that home ownership did increase among African Americans but not for all income levels. Overall, black home ownership rates increased from 43.7 percent to 46.6 percent between 1990 and 2000. White home ownership rates grew from 68.8 percent to 72.1 percent, yielding black-white home ownership ratios of .6354 in 1990 and .6462 in 2000. But, when comparing ownership rates with income cohorts, the black-white ratios did not improve in most cohorts and actually declined. Figure 6 illustrates this trend. Thus, within most income groups, blacks not only continued to be held to lower home ownership rates—the main source of African-American wealth—but actually lost ground relative to whites. The cause for alarm over this decline is that blacks hold more debt and fewer financial assets, according to the 2001 Survey of Consumer Finances. The result is that African Americans were less prepared to weather the bad times of the recession and have had greater difficulty taking advantage of the recovery and its associated benefits.

Poverty and Unemployment

In 2000, 3.79 million out of 21.16 million African Americans, aged 18 to 64, lived in poverty, producing a black poverty rate of 17.9 percent. The corresponding white poverty rate for that year was 6.7 percent. In 1992, 4.88 million blacks, 18 to 64 years old, lived in poverty. The respective black and white poverty rates for that year were 25.8 percent and 8.1 percent. Thus, the gap in poverty between blacks and whites narrowed over the decade. Black poverty was 3.18 times that of white poverty in 1992; it was 2.67 times that of white poverty in 2000.

Recent news accounts about the deepening of poverty during the post-9-11 era are born out by the statistics illustrated in Figure 7. In 2002, 4.28 million African Americans, 18 to 64 years of age, lived in poverty, an increase of 483,000 persons over 2000. This surge in poverty among working age blacks occurred during a period when white poverty also increased. As a result, poverty rates continued to narrow between working age blacks and whites.

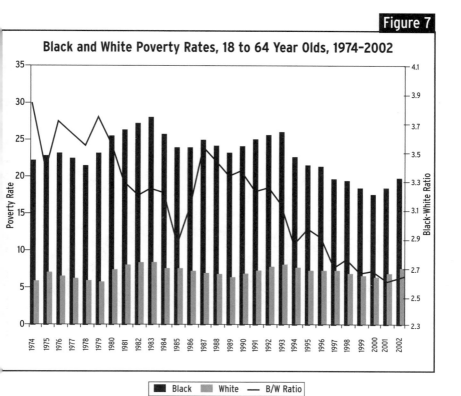

Figure 7

Black and White Poverty Rates, 18 to 64 Year Olds, 1974–2002

Black ■ White ■ — B/W Ratio

Just as black and white poverty rates declined during the decade, so did black and white unemployment rates. Indeed, black male unemployment rates fell to 5.9 percent in June 1999—lower than at any other point in the previous two decades. However, since white unemployment fell even more than black during the early years of the expansion the unemployment gap widened, then narrowed during the latter years of the 1990s and early 2000s. But, then, as Figure 8 also shows, a worsening of unemployment for blacks and whites at the onset of and during the recession caused the unemployment gap once again to widen. The ratio of black to white unemployment in June 1992 was 2.2. In June 1999 it was 1.96. But, in June 2000, the ratio rose again to 2.38. After falling at the beginning of the recession, it began to rise again and continued to rise well into the last months of 2003. Thus, the long period of expansion and improvement does not seem to have fostered a long-term or permanent narrowing of the male black-white unemployment gap.

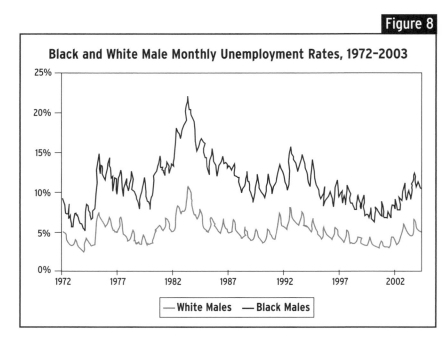

Figure 8

Black and White Male Monthly Unemployment Rates, 1972–2003

— White Males — Black Males

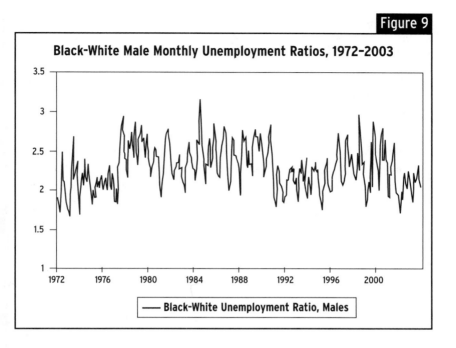

Figure 9

Black-White Male Monthly Unemployment Ratios, 1972–2003

— Black-White Unemployment Ratio, Males

Conclusion

African Americans benefited from the expansion of the economy during the past decade. Their household incomes increased and the income gap between blacks and whites narrowed somewhat. Black wage and salary gains were not as great, relative to those of whites, though. Unemployment fell faster for white males than for black males and resulted in a widening of unemployment gaps for this group during the expansion and recovery. Poverty rates declined and the general racial gaps in poverty narrowed up until the recession. In recent years, however, poverty rates are once again increasing among blacks and a new widening of the racial poverty gap has begun.

Although the boom brought increased incomes, higher levels of employment, and falling poverty rates for many African Americans, few were able to translate these income gains into permanent assets. Debt among blacks remains high—much higher than it is among whites. There is a paucity of financial assets, with blacks holding much of their wealth in their homes. Mortgage interest rates fell to unprecedented levels, but fewer and fewer African Americans applied for these conventional loans. Home ownership increased during the boom, but by the end of the decade, the black-white gap in home ownership persisted within different income ranges.

Thus, the boom benefited African Americans but black fortunes reversed quickly and decisively. Long-term improvements in the economic well-being of African Americans will not be sustained by the narrowing of income gaps alone. Until and unless black wealth increases faster than white wealth—black assets growing faster than white assets or black debt declining faster than white debt—there is little hope of a further narrowing of the racial gap in net worth.

Why do we care about net worth as a measure of economic well-being? During downturns, such as the one just experienced, high net worth is a key mechanism for weathering the storm. When African Americans move into high wage jobs, unexpected shocks to the economy—such as 9-11— can either have permanently debilitating effects or transitory effects depending on how well prepared they are. With income invested in financial assets along with ownership of property, black workers—even the lowest earning workers—can in effect insure against layoffs and unemployment. They are equipped to re-enter the market or even shift to other occupations through retraining and advanced education, if sufficient reserves exist from the boom times. Reserves also protect consumers who wish to take advantage of low prices that typically accompany temporary declines in the economy. For example, in some communities housing prices reached record lows and of course interest rates spiraled down to bargain-basement levels. But, without sufficient reserves, African-American families were unable to take advantage of these opportunities.

The lesson to be learned from the long period of expansion is that African American families and households still are perched precariously between a significant narrowing of income gaps and persistent inequality in wealth. As William Darity and I argued in our recent book, *Persistent*

Disparity: Race & Economic Inequality in the U.S. Since 1945, it is not obvious that current policies designed to remedy continuing racial disparities in income will have long-term impacts on disparities in wealth. Some of the responsibility for narrowing wealth inequality must rest with the black community itself. Debt is unacceptably high. Ownership of financial assets is low as compared to consumption of goods—such as depreciable assets like automobiles. But, responsibility also rests with industry and government that share some of the culpability for racial gaps in credit markets and entry points to acquisition of wealth. In an era when many state and local governments are abandoning programs designed to assist minority-owned businesses, there is no concomitant effort to eradicate the general societal conditions that lead to wide disparities in business ownership and ownership of other assets in the first place. The decade of the 1990s, then, provides a cautionary tale about how economic well-being of African Americans can appear to improve when in fact their relative position is about the same at the end of the decade as it was at the beginning of the decade.

Notes

[1]Seasonally adjusted unemployment rates for the civilian non-institutionalized population, 16 years and older.

[2]The source for these figures is the Current Population Survey, March Supplement. The March Supplement refers to income in the previous year. Thus, technically speaking, the income measures for 2000 refer to the period ending in December, 1999.

[3]Ana M. Aizcorbe, Arthur B. Kennickell, and Kevin B. Moore, "Recent Changes in U.S. Family Finances Evidence for the 1998 and 2001 Survey of Consumer Finances" Table 3, Federal Reserve Bulletin 89 (January 2003): 1-32.

[4]Source for wealth statistics is Arthur B. Kennickell, "A Rolling Tide: Changes in theDistribution of Wealth in the U.S., 1989-2001," November 2003, Working Paper No. 393, The Levy Economics Institute of Bard College.

[5]Kennickell, "A Rolling Tide," Table 24, p. 43.

[6]All mortgage lending figures were retrieved online using the Home Mortgage Disclosure Act (HMDA) National Aggregate Reports http://www.ffiec.gov/hmda_rpt/natagg_welcome.htm.

[7]Many loans are approved and not accepted by the applicant. This often occurs when applicants make multiple applications, but it also occurs when an applicant decides not to purchase the property for whatever reason. About 10 to 10.7 percent of black loan applications are approved by lenders but not accepted by loan applicants. The rate for whites was 9.6 percent in 1997 and 7.6 percent in 2002.

References

Aizcorbe, Ana M., Arthur B. Kennickell and Kevin B. Moore. 2003. "Recent Changes in U.S. Family Finances: Evidence for the 1998 and 2001 Survey of Consumer Finances." *Federal Reserve Bulletin 89(*January): 1-32.

Boushey, Heather and Robert Cherry. 2003. "The Severe Implications of the Economic Downturn on Working Families." *Working USA* 6 (3)(Winter 2002-3): 35-54.

Current Population Survey. 2001. March Supplement. A19.

Darity, Jr., William A. and Samuel L. Myers, Jr. 1998. *Persistent Disparity: Race & Economic Inequality in the U.S. Since 1945.* Northampton, MA: Edward Elgar Publishing.

Kennickell, Arthur B., Martha Starr-McCluer and Brian J. Surrette. 2000. "Recent Change in U.S. Family Finances: Results from the 1998 Survey of Consumer Finances." *Federal Reserve Bulletin(*January): 1-29. http://www.federalreserve.gov/pubs/bulletin/2000/0100lead.pdf

Kennickell, Arthur B. 2003. "A Rolling Tide: Changes in the Distribution of Wealth in the U.S., 1989-2001." Paper presented at the Levy Institute Conference on "International Perspectives on Household Wealth," October 17-18, 2003. The Levy Economics Institute of Bard College. http://www.federalreserve.gov/pubs/oss/oss2/papers/concentration.2001.9.pdf

TABLE 1: Average Wage and Salary Income (In Constant Dollars)
1 9 9 0

		Black Non-Hispanic	White Non-Hispanic	B/W Ratio
Total		$21,379.42 *45.22%*	$29,101.15 *52.37%*	73.47%
Married	*All*	$26,864.47 *71.42%*	$34,454.07 *66.34%*	77.97%
	Age < 30	$18,840.22 *81.43%*	$22,805.75 *83.21%*	82.61%
	Age 30 - 50	$29,172.82 *83.38%*	$37,394.72 *80.18%*	78.01%
	Age > 50	$26,983.10 *46.99%*	$35,788.93 *42.51%*	75.40%
Not Married	*All*	$17,606.25 *36.11%*	$21,062.82 *39.78%*	83.59%
	Age < 30	$11,776.01 *25.86%*	$13,505.48 *32.60%*	87.19%
	Age 30 - 50	$23,106.10 71.19%	$31,855.86 82.73%	72.53%
	Age > 50	$21,705.47 *32.14%*	$25,283.31 *28.53%*	85.85%
Male		$23,973.44 *46.76%*	$37,025.77 *57.57%*	64.75%
Married	*All*	$31,161.77 *75.22%*	$45,261.07 *73.56%*	68.85%
	Age < 30	$21,652.34 *88.01%*	$29,027.17 *92.63%*	74.59%
	Age 30 - 50	$33,665.39 *87.37%*	$49,515.93 *88.75%*	67.99%
	Age > 50	$31,214.86 *51.60%*	$45,144.62 *50.06%*	69.14%
Not Married	*All*	$17,938.84 *35.49%*	$23,264.99 *42.23%*	77.11%
	Age < 30	$12,243.32 *26.09%*	$14,699.73 *34.04%*	83.29%
	Age 30 -50	$23,980.08 *70.63%*	$35,956.38 *81.76%*	66.69%
	Age > 50	$25,693.66 *35.71%*	$34,971.06 *36.23%*	73.47%
Female		$18,919.46 *43.85%*	$19,945.95 *47.41%*	94.85%
Married	*All*	$20,398.60 *67.35%*	$20,775.00 *59.01%*	98.19%
	Age < 30	$16,144.28 *75.98%*	$17,158.69 *76.18%*	94.09%
	Age 30 - 50	$23,903.01 *79.14%*	$22,453.01 *71.64%*	106.46%
	Age > 50	$20,438.93 *41.28%*	$19,576.31 *33.69%*	104.41%
Not Married	*All*	$17,337.84 *36.62%*	$18,842.48 *37.58%*	92.01%
	Age < 30	$11,306.35 *25.64%*	$12,046.69 *31.00%*	93.85%
	Age 30 - 50	$22,481.78 *71.60%*	$27,843.62 *83.69%*	80.74%
	Age > 50	$19,693.27 *30.59%*	$20,687.82 *25.92%*	95.19%

Black Non-Hispanic	White Non-Hispanic	B/W Ratio
$24,847.89 **46.18%**	$34,273.19 **52.56%**	72.50%
$30,312.68 **69.86%**	$40,615.59 **66.19%**	74.63%
$19,867.50 **15.27%**	$24,240.13 **83.50%**	81.96%
$31,780.73 **63.51%**	$43,140.54 **81.30%**	73.67%
$33,434.23 **21.22%**	$42,662.59 **44.80%**	78.37%
$21,177.31 **37.61%**	$25,097.53 **40.49%**	84.38%
$13,428.08 **24.83%**	$14,476.07 **30.28%**	92.76%
$26,289.03 73.59%	$35,125.82 82.43%	74.84%
$27,484.96 **34.05%**	$31,828.08 **32.68%**	86.35%
$27,449.63 **45.44%**	$42,779.90 **56.66%**	64.16%
$33,988.90 **71.36%**	$52,396.54 **71.95%**	64.87%
$21,608.41 **74.77%**	$29,924.59 **91.30%**	72.21%
$35,655.53 **83.30%**	$55,835.02 **88.78%**	63.86%
$37,234.61 **50.32%**	$53,958.34 **50.36%**	69.01%
$21,673.00 **34.41%**	$27,569.39 **42.41%**	78.61%
$13,840.20 **22.86%**	$16,034.71 **31.09%**	86.31%
$27,575.51 **69.48%**	$38,640.56 **81.59%**	71.36%
$30,473.84 **36.25%**	$39,238.74 **39.89%**	77.66%
$22,577.56 **46.83%**	$24,764.12 **48.61%**	91.17%
$25,927.54 **68.16%**	$26,396.19 **60.36%**	98.22%
$18,019.61 **77.46%**	$19,059.78 **77.46%**	94.54%
$27,312.77 **79.41%**	$28,394.59 **74.06%**	96.19%
$27,963.41 **43.06%**	$25,874.06 **38.47%**	108.08%
$20,827.67 **40.26%**	$22,623.45 **38.73%**	92.06%
$13,081.88 **26.77%**	$12,676.44 **29.41%**	103.20%
$25,439.68 **76.59%**	$31,427.11 **83.35%**	80.95%
$25,976.81 **33.04%**	$27,512.49 **29.56%**	94.42%

B/W Ratio: Black/White

"Not Married" category includes divorced, separated, widowed, and never married. Percents under income are the ratios of the persons with positive income in the corresponding category.

Wage and salary incomes in 1990 were converted to constant 2000 dollars using Consumer Price Index (CPI, 1982-1984 = 100).

Only those who have positive wage and salary income are included in the mean calculation.

Source: 1% Public-Use Micro Data Sample (PUMS) Files for 1990 and 2000

TABLE 2: Average Home Ownership Rates

	1990		
	Black Non-Hispanic	White Non-Hispanic	B/W Ratio
Total	43.73%	68.82%	63.55%
Married *All*	62.60%	80.64%	77.63%
Age < 30	24.77%	48.77%	50.80%
Age 30–50	60.06%	80.66%	74.45%
Age > 50	79.52%	89.87%	88.48%
Not Married *All*	32.64%	51.36%	63.55%
Age < 30	8.74%	17.65%	49.50%
Age 30–50	28.01%	47.82%	58.58%
Age > 50	50.18%	67.00%	74.89%
Male Headed	53.69%	74.10%	72.45%
Married *All*	65.08%	81.27%	80.08%
Age < 30	26.75%	49.69%	53.83%
Age 30–50	62.42%	81.07%	76.99%
Age > 50	80.35%	90.02%	89.25%
Not Married *All*	32.61%	47.07%	69.27%
Age < 30	13.88%	21.41%	64.85%
Age 30–50	30.23%	48.01%	62.96%
Age > 50	45.82%	66.34%	69.06%
Female Headed	34.27%	56.50%	60.66%
Married *All*	48.08%	72.65%	66.18%
Age < 30	18.30%	42.16%	43.40%
Age 30–50	46.42%	75.56%	61.43%
Age > 50	72.96%	87.40%	83.48%
Not Married *All*	32.65%	53.81%	60.68%
Age < 30	6.74%	13.82%	48.82%
Age 30 - 50	27.15%	47.66%	56.98%
Age > 50	51.71%	67.22%	76.93%

2 0 0 0		
Black Non-Hispanic	White Non-Hispanic	B/W Ratio
46.61%	72.13%	64.63%
65.96%	84.82%	77.76%
29.86%	53.56%	55.76%
62.98%	84.09%	74.89%
80.73%	91.34%	88.38%
36.16%	55.54%	65.10%
12.59%	19.51%	64.55%
33.06%	53.00%	62.38%
52.28%	69.79%	74.91%
55.74%	77.39%	72.02%
69.86%	85.81%	81.41%
33.41%	55.00%	60.74%
66.26%	84.82%	78.12%
82.45%	91.67%	89.93%
35.14%	52.31%	67.17%
17.01%	22.85%	74.45%
33.35%	52.98%	62.94%
47.27%	68.35%	69.16%
38.64%	61.02%	63.33%
51.43%	76.19%	67.50%
23.60%	47.99%	49.18%
52.01%	78.38%	66.35%
70.23%	87.05%	80.67%
36.57%	57.64%	63.46%
10.80%	16.27%	66.38%
32.94%	53.02%	62.12%
54.22%	70.38%	77.04%

B/W Ratio: Black/White
Each category indicates marital status, gender, and age of a household head.
"Not Married" category includes divorced, separated, widowed, and never married.
Source: 1% Public-Use Micro Data Sample (PUMS) Files for 1990 and 2000

73

TABLE 3: Average Home Ownership Rates by Household Income Levels

1 9 9 0

	Black Non-Hispanic	White Non-Hispanic	B/W Ratio
Total	43.73% **0.4961**	68.82% **0.4632**	63.54%
under $25,000	31.87% **0.4660**	53.05% **0.4991**	60.08%
$25,000 to $50,000	45.44% **0.4979**	65.48% **0.4754**	69.40%
$50,000 to $75,000	60.73% **0.4884**	77.76% **0.4159**	78.10%
$75,000 to $100,000	74.34% **0.4368**	85.12% **0.3559**	87.34%
$100,000 to $125,000	81.39% **0.3892**	88.93% **0.3138**	91.52%
$125,000 to $150,000	82.80% **0.3774**	90.45% **0.2939**	91.54%
$150,000 and over	82.25% **0.3821**	91.65% **0.2766**	89.74%
Male Headed	53.69% **0.4986**	74.10% **0.4381**	72.46%
under $25,000	39.92% **0.4897**	56.93% **0.4952**	70.12%
$25,000 to $50,000	50.09% **0.5000**	68.70% **0.4637**	72.91%
$50,000 to $75,000	64.15% **0.4796**	79.97% **0.4002**	80.22%
$75,000 to $100,000	77.69% **0.4163**	86.77% **0.3388**	89.54%
$100,000 to $125,000	83.81% **0.3684**	90.00% **0.3000**	93.12%
$125,000 to $150,000	86.03% **0.3467**	91.25% **0.2826**	94.28%
$150,000 and over	85.15% **0.3556**	92.32% **0.2663**	92.23%
Female Headed	34.27% **0.4746**	56.50% **0.4958**	60.65%
under $25,000	27.69% **0.4475**	49.53% **0.5000**	55.91%
$25,000 to $50,000	39.72% **0.4893**	57.24% **0.4947**	69.39%
$50,000 to $75,000	53.08% **0.4991**	67.13% **0.4697**	79.07%
$75,000 to $100,000	63.59% **0.4812**	75.66% **0.4291**	84.05%
$100,000 to $125,000	72.87% **0.4446**	81.71% **0.3866**	89.18%
$125,000 to $150,000	70.34% **0.4568**	84.69% **0.3601**	83.06%
$150,000 and over	70.64% **0.4554**	86.50% **0.3417**	81.66%

	2000	
Black Non-Hispanic	**White** Non-Hispanic	**B/W Ratio**

Black Non-Hispanic	White Non-Hispanic	B/W Ratio
46.61% *0.4988*	72.13% *0.4484*	64.62%
31.53% *0.4646*	53.99% *0.4984*	58.40%
47.38% *0.4993*	68.46% *0.4647*	69.21%
63.71% *0.4808*	79.76% *0.4018*	79.88%
74.49% *0.4359*	86.18% *0.3451*	86.44%
79.30% *0.4052*	89.03% *0.3125*	89.07%
80.34% *0.3974*	89.66% *0.3045*	89.61%
78.51% *0.4108*	90.86% *0.2882*	86.41%
55.84% *0.4966*	77.39% *0.4183*	72.15%
37.26% *0.4835*	57.96% *0.4936*	64.29%
51.43% *0.4998*	71.71% *0.4504*	71.72%
67.07% *0.4700*	82.09% *0.3834*	81.70%
77.65% *0.4166*	87.93% *0.3258*	88.31%
83.07% *0.3750*	90.37% *0.2950*	91.92%
84.89% *0.3581*	91.31% *0.2817*	92.97%
85.32% *0.3539*	92.10% *0.2697*	92.64%
38.64% *0.4869*	61.02% *0.4877*	63.32%
28.70% *0.4524*	50.66% *0.5000*	56.65%
43.65% *0.4960*	61.80% *0.4859*	70.63%
58.24% *0.4932*	71.54% *0.4512*	81.41%
67.42% *0.4687*	78.06% *0.4138*	86.37%
69.30% *0.4612*	82.20% *0.3825*	84.31%
65.99% *0.4737*	82.64% *0.3788*	79.85%
62.08% *0.4852*	84.53% *0.3616*	73.44%

B/W Ratio: Black/White
Household incomes in 1990 were converted to constant 2000 dollars using the Consumer Price Index (CPI, 1982-1984 = 100).

Source: 1% Public-Use Micro Data Sample (PUMS) Files for 1990 and 2000. Standard errors of home ownership distribution in the corresponding household income categories are in italics.

Table 4: Average Wage and Salary Income by Industry

| | Manufacturing | | Service |
	Black Non-Hispanic	White Non-Hispanic	Black Non-Hispanic
All			
1990	$19,577.90	$27,756.10	$17,023.40
1991	$20,491.90	$28,722.60	$17,200.00
1992	$19,915.80	$30,155.40	$18,496.60
1993	$20,912.60	$30,996.30	$18,957.70
1994	$22,472.70	$32,251.30	$20,841.30
1995	$24,413.20	$35,886.60	$22,465.90
1996	$24,751.10	$36,876.20	$24,017.10
1997	$25,216.80	$38,598.20	$23,368.60
1998	$27,820.90	$40,382.60	$24,257.20
1999	$29,348.90	$41,775.80	$26,402.10
2000	$30,564.20	$45,871.90	$27,475.80
2001	$32,362.70	$46,462.70	$28,751.30
2002	$33,214.10	$46,227.90	$29,590.30
Male			
1990	$21,548.90	$31,968.20	$19,614.60
1991	$22,284.60	$32,789.40	$19,131.40
1992	$22,268.50	$34,194.50	$21,161.40
1993	$23,610.80	$34,683.50	$22,430.10
1994	$24,679.50	$36,489.80	$24,207.90
1995	$26,789.10	$40,794.90	$29,127.20
1996	$27,847.30	$41,700.30	$28,885.30
1997	$28,825.50	$43,867.90	$27,971.10
1998	$30,382.50	$45,733.90	$29,200.20
1999	$32,920.40	$47,228.50	$31,075.40
2000	$32,690.90	$52,611.70	$31,919.40
2001	$35,670.00	$51,179.80	$33,669.90
2002	$36,776.40	$51,129.10	$33,661.70

| Service | Retail | | Others | |
White Non-Hispanic	Black Non-Hispanic	White Non-Hispanic	Black Non-Hispanic	White Non-Hispanic
$23,203.90	$11,014.40	$16,284.10	$20,436.40	$26,867.90
$24,053.80	$11,992.00	$16,388.20	$20,661.70	$27,431.00
$24,949.50	$12,529.80	$17,295.90	$21,455.50	$28,522.60
$25,872.90	$12,717.90	$17,582.50	$22,676.90	$29,633.60
$26,879.20	$13,343.60	$18,796.80	$23,382.70	$30,449.90
$30,184.80	$14,767.20	$20,115.90	$23,179.30	$33,856.80
$30,901.90	$15,555.50	$21,371.50	$26,014.90	$35,833.70
$33,075.50	$16,210.10	$21,841.90	$26,702.40	$37,980.70
$35,289.10	$17,358.10	$23,807.60	$27,537.70	$39,307.10
$35,064.90	$17,853.80	$24,637.20	$29,920.90	$40,304.10
$38,523.90	$19,777.30	$26,857.40	$32,005.10	$44,304.20
$40,842.80	$18,893.90	$26,986.50	$33,378.00	$47,054.10
$40,168.10	$21,207.80	$29,905.00	$32,666.20	$46,363.20
$30,643.10	$13,342.70	$21,722.30	$20,395.20	$30,155.80
$31,539.20	$13,776.70	$21,489.70	$20,714.10	$30,603.10
$32,716.00	$14,208.60	$22,537.60	$21,397.10	$31,602.10
$33,626.50	$14,933.20	$22,983.90	$22,926.80	$33,108.10
$34,989.20	$15,232.80	$24,857.70	$24,201.20	$33,650.80
$41,022.30	$16,881.30	$26,381.90	$23,541.70	$38,349.50
$42,173.80	$17,731.10	$28,738.80	$26,200.80	$40,475.40
$45,011.70	$19,438.40	$29,039.20	$27,855.00	$42,812.00
$48,396.60	$21,647.50	$31,474.80	$27,792.70	$43,683.40
$47,482.60	$21,650.40	$32,754.20	$31,443.60	$45,259.40
$53,435.80	$23,730.10	$35,214.10	$35,792.70	$49,710.50
$56,153.30	$22,609.40	$34,633.10	$35,068.60	$52,539.90
$54,453.60	$24,525.50	$39,416.50	$35,010.40	$52,277.80

Table 4 continued on next page

TABLE 4: Average Wage and Salary Income by Industry

	Manufacturing		Service
	Black Non-Hispanic	White Non-Hispanic	Black Non-Hispanic
Female			
1990	$16,244.80	$18,798.20	$15,625.30
1991	$17,409.90	$20,027.40	$16,180.70
1992	$16,227.30	$21,001.60	$17,099.10
1993	$16,910.00	$22,495.20	$17,244.20
1994	$19,169.10	$22,593.80	$19,101.10
1995	$20,080.30	$24,745.70	$19,902.10
1996	$20,414.10	$26,118.00	$21,587.20
1997	$19,593.10	$26,594.60	$21,243.20
1998	$23,608.30	$27,958.80	$22,034.50
1999	$24,339.40	$29,869.60	$24,052.10
2000	$27,712.70	$31,144.80	$25,240.70
2001	$26,875.10	$33,153.40	$26,327.20
2002	$27,849.60	$33,848.30	$27,479.10

| Service | Retail | | Others | |
White Non-Hispanic	Black Non-Hispanic	White Non-Hispanic	Black Non-Hispanic	White Non-Hispanic
$18,277.30	$8,994.80	$11,387.20	$20,508.90	$20,046.80
$19,110.80	$10,259.80	$11,934.20	$20,565.10	$20,901.50
$19,843.60	$10,705.60	$12,653.80	$21,563.30	$22,217.40
$20,712.20	$10,439.60	$12,759.40	$22,214.40	$22,684.70
$21,574.60	$11,432.50	$13,317.10	$21,857.90	$23,729.90
$22,975.60	$12,679.50	$14,439.90	$22,514.30	$24,517.30
$23,669.90	$13,736.30	$14,670.50	$25,687.70	$26,037.70
$25,260.60	$13,181.50	$15,453.30	$24,853.80	$28,215.40
$26,742.30	$13,209.00	$16,908.20	$26,792.30	$29,715.70
$27,025.10	$14,319.10	$16,997.10	$27,428.60	$30,369.90
$28,795.60	$16,136.90	$18,851.90	$26,175.20	$32,272.90
$31,082.80	$15,397.60	$19,605.50	$30,647.60	$35,846.90
$30,970.00	$17,630.90	$20,394.90	$29,202.70	$34,313.10

Source: CPS March Supplement Files (http://dataferrett.census.gov)

Note: All are 20 years old and over, positive earners.
In 2002, black non-Hispanic is defined as black only and multi with black.

Brown at 50: Considering the Continuing Legal Struggle for Racial Justice

By Charles J. Ogletree, Jr.

On May 17, 1954, fifteen months into Dwight D. Eisenhower's presidency, Chief Justice Earl Warren, speaking on behalf of a unanimous Supreme Court, issued a historic ruling that he and his colleagues hoped would irrevocably change the social fabric of the United States. In the collection of cases known as *Brown v. Board of Education of Topeka* challenging the legality of racial segregation in public schooling, Warren declared, "We conclude that in the field of public education the doctrine of 'separate but-equal' has no place. Separate educational facilities are inherently unequal."[1] Thurgood Marshall, who had passionately argued the case before the Court, joined a jubilant throng of fellow civil rights leaders in hailing this decision as the Court's most significant opinion of the twentieth century. The *New York Times* extolled the *Brown* decision as having "reaffirmed its faith and the underlying American faith in the equality of all men and all children before the law." But when the *Brown* litigants returned in 1955 to address specific questions concerning the scope of the initial ruling, the Court concluded that, to achieve the goal of desegregation, the lower federal courts were to "enter such orders and decrees consistent with this opinion as are necessary and proper to admit to public schools on a racially nondiscriminatory basis with all deliberate speed the parties to these cases."[2]

As Thurgood Marshall and other civil rights lawyers pondered what the Court meant in adding the crucial phrase "all deliberate speed" to its opinion, a staff member reportedly consulted a dictionary to confirm their worst fears—that the "all deliberate speed" language meant "slow" and thus that the apparent victory of Brown was compromised because it effectively meant resisters were to be allowed to end segregation on their own timetable.

These three critical words would indeed turn out to be of great consequence, in that they ignored the urgency on which the *Brown* lawyers insisted. When asked to explain his view of "all deliberate speed," Thurgood Marshall frequently spelled out the word: S-L-O-W.[3]

Thurgood Marshall's perception was prophetic: the as-yet unfinished process of implementing *Brown* has turned out to be nearly as slow as the process of tearing down the Jim Crow system that allowed the educational segregation challenged in *Brown*.

Segregation grew out of white resistance to black emancipation after the Civil War. The newly freed African-Americans sought inclusion in a wage labor system that respected their transformed status as laborers and citizens who had the same legal rights and privileges as whites. But southern whites clung to the old paternalistic myths justifying slavery, declaring themselves "protectors of southern blacks and regarding their former slaves as ignorant and now resentful children. Newly freed African Americans were prohibited from participating on equal terms with whites in the labor market.

In the political sphere, additional barriers were erected to prevent the recently freed slaves from enjoying many of the rights of citizenship. In an 1873 decision in three cases known collectively as the *Slaughter-House Cases*, the Supreme Court effectively created two tiers of citizenship by interpreting the Fourteenth Amendment to guarantee the "privileges and immunities" of citizenship nationally, as enforced by the federal government, but not locally in the individual states.[4] That meant states could now determine the citizenship status of those who lived within their jurisdiction, and many in the South and border regions set to work creating a second-class citizenship for African Americans. In 1883 in a number of consolidated cases known as the *Civil Rights Cases*, the Court introduced the non-constitutional concept of "state action" to undermine the Fourteenth Amendment's reach beyond governments into the actions of individuals. Effectively, the Court refused to outlaw private acts of discrimination, thus setting the stage for the legalized segregation that became known as Jim Crow. At the state level, whites in control of local and state governments and private businesses and institutions quickly seized on the Court's permitting a two-tiered system of justice to disenfranchise African Americans. Voting rights were removed by a variety of means, most notoriously by the "grandfather clauses" that required voters to be descended from individuals who were citizens of the states during slavery. That effectively removed most African-Americans from the voting rolls.[5]

As the reign of Jim Crow, with its attendant extra-legal violence, deepened, African Americans slowly reconstructed both a powerful sense of determination to challenge their legal oppression as well as institutions, such as the National Association for the Advancement of Colored People, to shape and direct it. The NAACP's efforts to plan new legal strategies to defeat Jim Crow and overturn its most infamous legal bulwark, the Supreme Court's 1896 decision in *Plessy v. Ferguson*, began to build to victory in the 1920s and 1930s when Charles Hamilton Houston, an African-American graduate of Harvard Law School, began to contribute his estimable legal brilliance to the challenge.

By the mid-1930s, Houston, having spent several years in private practice in Washington, D.C., and then as a professor and dean at Howard Law School, took over and fleshed out the NAACP's three-prong litigation strategy: first, solidifying a nationwide network of African-American lawyers to file "test case" suits against segregation practices; second, building precedential support for a direct constitutional attack against segregation through this carefully targeted litigation; and third, organizing local black communities to support legal, political, and social action against ongoing discriminatory practices. To Houston, the legal campaign was part of a greater national effort to mobilize the black community against segregation.[6]

At Houston's direction, the tight-knit network of lawyers spread across the country began to find the plaintiffs who would bring the suits to chip away at segregation's legal bulwarks. Their participation, largely given *pro bono,* was crucial, for they were, in effect, the NAACP's local militia—legal advocate foot soldiers in the national office's strategic campaign.

Intent on establishing key precedents that would lay the groundwork for an eventual direct attack on segregation, Houston carefully selected a few target areas for the litigation campaign. He first resolved that he wanted to concentrate the litigation effort on segregation and inequities in education. Himself the product of a first-rate education (he had graduated at the top of his class from both Washington's Dunbar High School and Amherst College), he saw quality education as the essential preparation for life and believed that poor, inadequate schools placed a lifelong handicap on many American blacks, both in competing economically and in seeking equal rights. To him, segregation and inequities in American schools represented the worst symptom of American racism. Thus, he decided the NAACP should focus exclusively on three kinds of school desegregation cases: suits seeking the desegregation of state-run graduate and professional schools, suits seeking to equalize the salary discrepancies between black and white teachers, and suits seeking to equalize the disparate physical facilities for black and white elementary and secondary schools.[7]

As part of their mobilizing efforts, Houston and his star pupil from Howard Law School, Thurgood Marshall, went on proselytizing campaigns throughout the South, building organizational support while arousing interest in forming plaintiffs' classes. Houston wrote a number of articles and pamphlets instructing communities how to bring lawsuits, build community solidarity, and agitate for better schools. This literature also explained how the equalization lawsuits were part of a greater strategic plan to attack educational segregation specifically and fight institutional racism generally. Most of all, Houston emphasized that while "the NAACP stands ready with advice and assistance" ultimately "the decision for action rests with the local community itself."[8]

II.

When *Brown* was litigated—without Houston, who had become ill and died of heart failure in April, 1950—the argument presented by Thurgood

Marshall and the other *Brown* lawyers persuaded the Supreme Court of the magnitude of the problem and led Chief Justice Earl Warren, writing for the unanimous Court, to conclude:

Today, education is perhaps the most important function of state and local governments... Today it is a principal instrument in awakening the child to cultural values, in preparing him for later professional training, and in helping him to adjust normally to his environment. In these days, it is doubtful that any child may reasonably be expected to succeed in life if he is denied the opportunity of an education. Such an opportunity, where the state has undertaken to provide it, is a right, which must be made available to all on equal terms. We come then to the question presented: Does segregation of children in public schools solely on the basis of race, even though the physical facilities and other "tangible" factors may be equal, deprive the children of the minority group of equal educational opportunities? We believe that it does. [9]

The Court's decision recognized the negative impact of segregation on black children in America and saw quality education as the appropriate means for beginning to eliminate the crippling effects of segregation. The Court applied these principles to the schools in question, but made it clear that the mandate applied to any school system with similar practices. During oral arguments, the justices asked the lawyers probing questions, giving little indication of where they were leaning. Justice Felix Frankfurter seemed particularly interested in how a decree would be implemented if the Court were to rule that segregation was unconstitutional. The *Brown* lawyers recognized the Court's concern with, and indeed "fear" over, the implementation of a Court decree abolishing segregation, specifically noting that this "fear" was the most "persuasive factor" working for the other side.

After each day of oral arguments, the *Brown* lawyers considered the justices' line of questioning, trying to discern which way the decision might come out. By the last day of argument, however, the lawyers were

TOLLESTON

not quite sure how the justices would rule. Indeed, on June 8, 1953, instead of issuing its opinion in *Brown*, the Court ordered that the cases be reargued. Even more surprising, it asked each side to answer five specifically targeted questions, the final two of which dealt with the Court's concern about the implementation of a decree mandating integration. Specifically, the Court wanted to know, if it overruled *Plessy v. Ferguson*, should black students "forthwith be admitted to schools of their choice" or should the Court allow for a "gradual adjustment."

On September 8, 1953, before the second round of oral arguments, Chief Justice Fred Vinson died, and President Eisenhower appointed Earl Warren the new Chief Justice. Upon hearing of his colleague's death, Frankfurter—presumably relieved at the removal of a possible obstacle to a favorable outcome in the case—is reported to have said, "This is the first indication I have had that there is a God."[10]

President Eisenhower's appointment of Warren, who had been the California attorney general and then the governor of that state, did not suggest a change of course for the Court. Warren, after all, was the attorney general who had defended the result in *Korematsu v. United States*, the 1944 case that ratified the policy of interning Japanese Americans during World War II, which was authored by another still-sitting justice, the Alabaman Hugo Black.[11]

However, what most observers, Eisenhower included, did not fully realize was that *Korematsu* had troubled Warren and that, as a Californian, he was considered to be a moderate Republican. Warren immediately recognized the importance of the *Brown* case and began an effort to persuade all of his colleagues to reach a unanimous decision. By May 17, 1954, the day the *Brown* ruling was handed down, he had his unanimity. But it was forged at a cost that would prove to be exceedingly high.

III.

In a break with tradition, the Court did not order the states to enforce the rights just announced. Instead, having broadly proclaimed its support of desegregating public schools, it instructed the *Brown* lawyers to return a few months later to address specific questions concerning the scope of their ruling. Their second ruling—*Brown II*—would legitimize much of the social upheaval that followed.

Fearful that segregationists within and outside the executive and legislative branches of state governments (and perhaps the federal government as well) would resist the decision, the Court offered a palliative to the opposition. Speaking again with one voice, the Court concluded that, to achieve the goal of desegregation, the lower federal courts were to "enter such orders and decrees consistent with this opinion as are necessary and proper to admit to public schools on a racially nondiscriminatory basis *with all deliberate speed* the parties to these cases."

As Thurgood Marshall and his colleagues understood immediately, this meant "slow." *Brown II* gave much of the discretion on how to carry out desegregation to federal district judges; but for more than a decade neither the Supreme Court nor the federal government gave them clear direction regarding desegregation.[12] Although federal judges were supposed to be protected from political pressures, the district courts at issue were located in communities in which "the segregated way of life was deemed very close to godliness."[13] Moreover, one could hardly expect these federal district courts to order immediate desegregation when the Supreme Court could not, and President Eisenhower strove mightily to follow a policy of nonintervention on desegregation. As a result, many federal courts in the South delayed desegregation cases for long periods, and then ordered only limited changes.

Under President Johnson, Washington finally began to use its power to vigorously enforce desegregation, and rapid and dramatic changes were realized in the South. The federal rules implementing the legislation became effective in 1965, and Justice Department civil rights lawyers began filing suits, proving that the sanctions imposed by law and cutoffs to federal aid were effective tools against school districts that refused to desegregate.

However, this commitment lasted only until President Nixon took office in 1969. During his presidential campaign, Nixon had curried favor with white voters, asserting a full fifteen years after *Brown II* that the courts had tried to force integration "too far too fast" and strongly implying he would take the lead in undoing busing policies.[14] Nixon did vigorously oppose the *Swann v. Charlotte-Mecklenburg Board of Education* decision, which ruled that busing was an appropriate means of achieving desegregation, and he supported congressional action to limit urban desegregation, including a constitutional amendment, if necessary.[15]

Any 1960s momentum to implement *Brown* truly stopped with the Court's decision in *Milliken v. Bradley*,[16] the first major post-*Brown* Supreme Court move against school desegregation. In *Milliken*, the Court was faced with the most basic barrier to school desegregation, especially in northern urban areas—white suburbanization. In many districts, there were not enough white students for a sustainable program of desegregation. A lower court had approved a plan of desegregation that would go beyond the city (Detroit, in this case) and into the surrounding suburbs. Five justices—four of them appointed by Nixon—found that the plan unfairly punished the suburbs and contradicted longstanding principles of local control over schools. Without any discriminatory suburban or state action, relief that had a punitive effect on the suburbs could not be granted.

In 1978 in the *Bakke Case*, Thurgood Marshall, then eleven years on the Court, would find himself sitting as a Supreme Court Justice in a lawsuit that called the *Brown* case into question, and that squarely raised the issue of what public institutions could do, or not do, to increase the deplorably low representation of minorities in their universities and graduate schools. Allan Bakke, a white student who had applied to the University of California at Davis Medical School and been rejected, filed a suit challenging an admissions program that affirmatively recruited and admitted African-American and Chicano applicants. Having lost in the lower Courts, the University of California had appealed to the Supreme Court, and more than fifty groups, including several universities and organizations such as the NAACP and American Civil Liberties Union, submitted *amicus curiae* briefs. The vast majority of the briefs supported the University of California's special admissions program.

For Marshall, the *Bakke* arguments must have been particularly poignant. In his view, the principle of color-blindness could not yet work, because for too many years the laws had specifically disadvantaged African Americans on account of their race. In an April 13, 1978 memorandum to his fellow Justices regarding the case, Justice Marshall wrote, "For us now to say that the principle of colorblindness prevents the University from giving 'special' consideration to race when this Court, in 1896 licensed the states to continue to consider race, is to make a mockery of the principle of equal justice under law."[17] Marshall asserted that the racial discrimination that had been upheld and promoted at every level of society between *Plessy* and *Brown* meant that many more years would have to pass before African Americans could gain equal footing with whites. He thus saw no need for a specific showing of past discrimination at Davis, because the discrimination was endemic in the nation and intrinsic to its institutions. He went on to declare, "If you view the program as admitting qualified students who, because of this Nation's sorry history of racial discrimination, have academic records that prevent them from effectively competing for medical school, then this is affirmative action to remove the vestiges of slavery and state imposed segregation by 'root and branch.'"[18]

To the other justices, however, the exclusion of white students without more justification was simply going too far. Indeed, Chief Justice Warren Burger and the eventual swing vote, Justice Lewis Powell, did focus on who was being kept out of Davis. This was not surprising, since Bakke himself was a very sympathetic character. For this very reason, Justice William Brennan was strongly against granting certiorari in the *Bakke* case. He feared that a majority of the Court would be offended by the existence of a "quota" and strike down any use of race in admissions programs. But the Justices did accept the case and, with Justice Powell writing for the majority, concluded that, although achieving a diverse student body constituted a compelling state interest, the California program was not narrowly tailored to meet that end.[19] However, he did uphold that facet of the University's plan which allowed the institution to consider diversity as one factor in selecting a class of students. Justices Brennan, White, Marshall, and Blackmun co-authored an opinion concurring with Justice Powell in the dissolution of the lower court's injunction against all consideration of race but dissenting from the invalidation of California's program. They considered Davis's interest in remedying past societal discrimination sufficiently important such that its admissions procedures neither stigmatized a discrete group or individual nor used race unreasonably.[20] Justice Stevens, joined by Chief Justice Burger and Justices Stewart and Rehnquist, concluded that the question of whether race could ever be considered was not before the Court, and he concurred in Justice Powell's opinion insofar as it held that Title VI invalidated the program and compelled admission of *Bakke*.

IV.

When I read the *Bakke* decision and its conclusion that race, as one factor among many, was appropriate for a university to consider in selecting from among qualified applicants, I was euphoric. All of our marching, protests, and my visits with the lawyers arguing the case, and attendance at the Supreme Court argument seemed to have been vindicated. However, I then read Justice Marshall's dissent in the case; it immediately caused me to reassess whether we had indeed prevailed in the *Bakke* case. Perhaps my glee was premature. I read Marshall's words very carefully and learned a lot about myself that day. Marshall filed a dissenting opinion arguing, "It must be remembered that, during most of the past 200 years, the Constitution as interpreted by this Court did not prohibit the most ingenious and pervasive forms of discrimination against the Negro. Now, when a State acts to remedy the effects of that legacy of discrimination, I cannot believe that this same Constitution stands as a barrier."[21] Marshall went on to recount the long and shameful history of American racism, including the Court's role in affirming the status of slaves as noncitizens and later in emasculating the Civil War amendments.[22] He concluded, "In light of the sorry history of discrimination and its devastating impact on the lives of Negroes, bringing the Negro into the mainstream of American life should be a state interest of the highest order. To fail to do so is to ensure that America will forever remain a divided society."[23]

It was ironic, in some respects, that I was graduating from a premier law school, on my way to a job I desperately wanted, and Marshall was signaling to me, and others like me, that our modest success paled in comparison with the closing of the doors of opportunity for other blacks, Native Americans, and Hispanics throughout the country. It was not enough that the Harvards and Stanfords were doing well, if the public institutions of higher education were starting to shut their doors.

V.

A number of arguments have been made about the deficiencies of *Bakke's* diversity rationale. First, it is a poor justification for affirmative action because it becomes less persuasive as the percentage of minority students grows—there are diminishing marginal returns in terms of racial diversity once the number reaches a certain point. This disjunction between how many minority students represent a critical mass, in contrast to the modest allowance that was envisioned by *Bakke*, makes post-*Bakke* policies look more like a commitment to getting to a certain number of minority students for each class than like loyalty to diversity. This is not really troublesome on its own, but it has certainly complicated recent efforts to argue that post-*Bakke* programs are narrowly tailored.

Professor Charles Lawrence argues that promotion of the "liberal defense of affirmative action," or more precisely the diversity defense first articulated by Powell in *Bakke*, has crowded out "more radical substantive defenses."[24] He holds that not only must defenders of affirmative action explain how traditional admissions standards continue to perpetuate racial and class-based privilege; they must also emphasize how past and current discrimination makes affirmative action necessary. Lawrence characterizes the diversity defense as essentially conservative because it only seeks to integrate existing black elites into current power structures as opposed to putting the goal of racial justice at the forefront of the university's mission. Similarly, Professor Lani Guinier argues that proponents of affirmative action need to reclaim the debate by directly contesting the misconception that "affirmative action is a departure from an otherwise sound meritocracy."[25] She claims that traditional admissions criteria disadvantage not only women and people of color but also the poor and working class. In other words, some scholars and others believe *Bakke* marked the end of the Supreme Court's receptiveness to potentially radical legal challenges to the status quo. Before *Bakke*, the Supreme Court recognized that the playing field was not level, but had been skewed in favor of whites and consistently took steps to remedy the inequality. After *Bakke*, it abandoned its attempts to re-balance the playing field by lifting African Americans, women, and others to the same level as white men.

I share the concerns of both Lawrence and Guinier. The Supreme Court's failure in *Bakke* to accept the University of California's efforts to remedy the dearth of minorities in professional schools was unwise and unfortunate. With one decision, the Court accelerated the process of undoing *Brown*.

VI.

By the time of last year's decisions in the affirmative action cases involving the University of Michigan Law School and its undergraduate program, much had changed since I had witnessed the *Bakke* argument before the Court. Now, I participated in a panel discussion the weekend before the argument, led by some of my former Harvard law students, who organized it, and a group of Howard law students, who hosted it. This time was also different in that two Ogletrees were attending the argument. My daughter, Rashida, a first-year law student at New York University, had joined other law students who took an overnight bus to D.C. to participate in the protests outside the Supreme Court. For me, it was a moment of joy to see my daughter, who was born one year after the *Bakke* decision, fighting for the future of affirmative action and participating in a protest march with her dad at the Supreme Court.

In *Gratz v. Bollinger* and *Grutter v. Bollinger*,[26] the Supreme Court answered the central question, debated since *Bakke*, of the propriety of university or college affirmative action programs. The results were, at best, a moderate success for affirmative action. They remain, in the context of the Court's jurisprudence on race- and economic-based educational programs, an important setback to the mission established in

Brown. Nonetheless, it was a day to celebrate, largely because a contrary decision in the law school case would have been unfathomable.

In *Grutter,* Justice Sandra Day O'Connor presented a robust endorsement of the principle of diversity as a factor in university admissions. In *Bakke,* Justice Powell emphasized that nothing less than the "nation's future depends upon leaders trained through wide exposure to the ideas and mores of students as diverse as this Nation of many peoples."[27] So long as the admissions program does not constitute the type of quota system of "racial balancing" outlawed by *Bakke,* it may admit a "critical mass" of minority students in an effort to obtain a racially diverse student body. Last year in the Michigan cases, Justice O'Connor not only endorsed Justice Powell's broad mandate, but went even further in embracing the significance of diversity.[28] In the *Gratz* opinion, Chief Justice Rehnquist, writing for a 6-to-3 majority, found the undergraduate admissions program unconstitutional. The chief justice found that awarding a blanket score—in this case, 20 points, or just over 13 percent of the maximum 150 points used to rank applicants—ensured that the university would admit all qualified minority applicants.

Collectively, *Grutter* and *Gratz* preserved the institution of affirmative action in American higher education and, to that extent, are important. Nonetheless, both cases—*Grutter* by what it did not say and *Gratz* by what it *did* say—are troubling in that they will likely fail to be the catalysts for dispensing with the "all deliberate speed" mentality adopted in *Brown.* With the decisions, the Court did not erect a further barrier in the path of the struggle to true integration and equality; it also did little to promote that struggle.

Justice O'Connor's opinion provided more than an answer to the mere question of *whether* the Michigan diversity plan was constitutional. She and a majority of her colleagues agreed that it was, but she went on to suggest *when* the diversity rationale would no longer find support from the Court: "It has been 25 years since Justice Powell first approved the use of race to further an interest in student body diversity in the context of public higher education. Since that time, the number of minority applicants with high grades and test scores has indeed increased. We expect that 25 years from now, the use of racial preferences will no longer be necessary to further the interest approved today."[29]

O'Connor's message in *Grutter* seems clear: the Court's decision does not solve the problem the Court addressed; it merely prolongs it. Although her support for the concept is unmistakable, her tolerance of long-term reliance on almost any rationale that focuses on race is limited. Her twenty-five-year sunset clause on diversity can properly be viewed as a challenge to the institutions of higher education, as well as the actual beneficiaries of such policies, to a make a serious effort to reach the goal of a color-blind society. For civil rights advocates and supporters of affirmative action, her sunset provision, eerily similar to Justice Powell's equally limited commitment to the diversity principle, holds the potential of being at once the most problematic and the most promising aspect of her opinion. Her challenge is problematic in that the opinion effectively dictates that affirmative action policies be considered merely temporary and in that it sets a window for achieving the elimination of affirmative action that is, when considered in the context of the centuries of *de jure* and *de facto* discrimination that preceded (and even followed) *Brown*, relatively short in time.

Lamenting the Court's adherence to strict scrutiny and the nation's sorry history on integration, Justice Ginsburg was on target: "It is well documented that conscious and unconscious race bias, even rank discrimination based on race, remain alive in our land, impeding realization of our highest values and ideals. . . . However strong the public's desire for improved education systems may be, . . . it remains the current reality that many minority students encounter markedly inadequate and unequal educational opportunities. . . . From today's vantage point, one may hope, but not firmly forecast, that over the next generation's span, progress toward nondiscrimination and genuinely equal opportunity will make it safe to sunset affirmative action."[30]

While the clock has already started running out on the future of affirmative action, Ginsburg reminds us that all of society must contribute to the change required to meet that deadline and fulfill the promise of *Brown*—and it will not be met without significant investment and effort toward the achievement of equal opportunity.

Notes

[1]*Brown v. Board of Education*, 347 U.S. 483, 495 (1954).

[2]*Brown v. Board of Education*, 349 U.S. 294, 301 (1955).

[3]James T. Patterson, Brown v. Board of Education: *Civil Rights Milestone and Its Troubled Legacy* (2001).

[4]*Slaughter-House Cases*, 83 U.S. 36, 71 (1873).

[5]John Hope Franklin and Alfred A. Moss, Jr., *From Slavery to Freedom: A History of African Americans*, 8th ed. (New York: Alfred A. Knopf, 2000), 288.

[6]Genna Rae McNeil, *Groundwork: Charles Hamilton Houston and the Struggle for Civil Rights* (Philadelphia: Univ. of Pennsylvania Press, 1983), 115–16.

[7]Mark Tushnet, T*he NAACP's Legal Strategy Against Segregated Education, 1925–1950* (Chapel Hill: Univ. of North Carolina Press, 1987), 34.

[8] Ibid., 44.

[9]*Brown*, 347 U.S. 483, 493.

[10]Morton J. Horwitz, *The Warren Court and the Pursuit of Justice* (New York: Hill and Wang, 1999).

[11] *Korematsu v. United States*, 323 U.S. 214, 215 (1944).

[12] J. W. Peltason, *Fifty-eight Lonely Men: Southern Federal Judges and School Desegregation* (New York: Harcourt, Brace and World, 1961), 4.

[13]Derrick Bell, "Heretical Thoughts on a Serious Occasion," in Brown *Plus Thirty: Perspectives on Desegregation*, ed. LaMar P. Miller (New York: Metropolitan Center for Educational Research, 1986), 70.

[14]Gary Orfield and Susan E. Eaton, *Dismantling Desegregation: The Quiet Reversal of Brown v. Board of Education* (New York: New Press, 1996), 8 – 9.

[15]Ibid., 9.

[16]*Milliken v. Bradley*, 418 U.S. 717 (1974).

[17]Bernard Schwartz, *Behind Bakke: Affirmative Action and the Supreme Court* (New York: New York Univ. Press, 1988), 238.

[18]Ibid., 128.

[19]*Bakke*, 438 U.S. 265, 310–15 (1978).

[20]Justice White wrote a separate opinion, arguing that there was no private right of action under Title VI. Ibid., 379–87. Justice Blackmun also wrote a separate opinion. Ibid. 402.

[21] Ibid., 387 (Marshall, J., concurring in part and dissenting in part).

[22] Ibid., 387– 94.

[23] Ibid., 396.

[24]Charles Lawrence, "Two Views of the River: A Critique of the Liberal Defense of Affirmative Action," *Columbia Law Review* 101 (2001): 928, 930.

[25]Susan Sturm and Lani Guinier, "The Future of Affirmative Action: Reclaiming the Innovative Ideal," *California Law Review 84* (1996): 953, 956.

[26]Gratz, 123 S.Ct. 2411 (2003); Grutter, 123 S. Ct. 2325 (2003).

[27]*Bakke*, 438 U.S. at 313.

[28]*See Grutter*, 123 S.Ct. at 2326.

[29]Ibid., 1247.

[30]Ibid., 1147–48 (Ginsburg, J., concurring).

The State of Education in Black America

By Edmund W. Gordon

Educational opportunities and academic achievement for some persons of African descent in the United States appear to be on the rise, judging from several of the findings outlined by the National Center for Education Statistics' (Hoffman, Lieges, & Snyder 2003) Report, *Status and Trends in the Education of Blacks.* The percentage of black children whose mothers have obtained a high school education has increased significantly since 1974. It also appears that more black students have completed high school and gone on to college. A significant number of us hold faculty appointments in non-historically black institutions. We seem to have reached a plateau, however, with respect to gains made in the 1960s, 70s and 80s in academic achievement. Hoffman, Lieges, and Snyder (2003) findings include:

- Black Children are more likely than white or Hispanic children to be enrolled in center-based preprimary education at the ages of 3, 4, and 5.

- Most black students attend public schools where minorities represent the majority of the student body. Seventy-three percent of black fourth-grade students were enrolled in schools with more than one-half of the students eligible to receive a free or reduced price lunch.

- Long-term trends in the scores of the National Assessment for Educational Progress show increased performance in reading for black students between 1971 and 1999. Trends in black performance in NAEP mathematics and sciences also show improvements over the long term.

- While black high school graduates completed more academic courses in 1998 than in 1982, their academic credit totals remained lower than those of whites in 1998. However, blacks' vocational credit totals were higher than those of whites.

- In 1998, black students were less likely than white students to take advanced mathematics courses and some advanced science courses and less likely than Hispanic students to take advanced foreign language classes. Between 1984 and 2000, the number of black students per 1000 twelfth graders taking Advanced Placement (AP) examinations increased. However, fewer black students per 1000 twelfth graders than white or Hispanic students took AP exams in 2000.

- In 1999, a lower percentage of black and Hispanic children than white children were in private schools.

- In 1999-2000, the proportion of associate degrees earned by blacks was greater than the proportion of bachelor's degrees earned by blacks.

- Nearly one-quarter of all bachelor's degrees earned by blacks in 1999 were earned at Historically Black Colleges and Universities.

- The proportion of blacks completing college increased between 1975 and 2000; however blacks still remained less likely than whites to earn degrees.

- In 1999, black instructional faculty in colleges and universities were more likely to be assistant professors than professors or associate professors.

With regards to the sciences and engineering, African-American students earned only 2,149 bachelor's degrees in Social Science; 4,851 degrees in Biological/Life Sciences; and 4,324 degrees in Engineering for the year 2000-2001 (American Council on Education's *Minorities in Higher Education, 2002-2003. Twentieth Annual Status Report,* 2003).

On the graduate level, it is also alarming that African Americans earned only 80 degrees in Physical Science; 190 degrees in Life Science; 299 degrees in Social Science; and 82 degrees in Engineering (American Council on Education's *Minorities in Higher Education, 2002-2003. Twentieth Annual Status Report,* 2003). These figures are cause for concern because African-American students represent approximately 11 percent of all students enrolled in higher education (American Council on Education's *Minorities in Higher Education, 1999-2000. Seventeenth Annual Status Report, 2000*). This reality is of particular concern not just for the gifted and talented African-American students who do not persist and graduate in the sciences, but also for higher education and the nation, which increasingly rewards those skills and intellectual competencies required for meaningful participation in an advanced technological society. These include the ability to bring order to the chaos created by information overload; the ability to reason; uncover relationships between phenomena; and use comparison, context, intent and values in arriving at judgments. Indeed, the capacity to function effectively in these domains is the essence of intellectual competence, increasingly the universal currency in technologically advanced societies.

It is difficult, if not impossible, to understand the current status of the education of blacks in the United States or the nature of the challenge of its improvement without an appreciation of the social, cultural, political and economic contexts in which the processes of education occur.

Context of Achievement Disparities

Available research continues to reinforce the idea that attempts at reducing achievement disparities among minority groups must seriously take into account the range of challenges that disadvantaged children, their families, and the schools that serve them, constantly encounter. Family and school instability, for example, ranks high among the research-based findings of poverty-related barriers. Indeed, disadvantaged families are (1) more likely to move often, especially in urban areas, and (2) may not be aware that these school changes may interfere with their children's education. For students who are more settled, however, learning is disrupted by frequent changes in the composition of their classroom. Effective teaching is also compromised by the presence and high turnover rate of inexperienced and unqualified teachers. Given that Latinos (who now make up the largest minority group), and blacks make up a disproportionate number of disadvantaged students, this issue becomes even more problematic because the effects of "poverty on racial and ethnic achievement gaps...will continue to be substantial" (The College Board 1999).

Another factor affecting the racial and ethnic achievement gap revolves around variation in the education levels of minority parents. Unlike parents with a high school education or less, most parents with college degrees understand and emphasize academic achievement by supplementing their children's education with travel, dance lessons, scouting, tutoring, summer camp, etc. Indeed, informed parents, scholars, and educators have known for some time now that schools alone cannot enable or ensure high academic achievement (Coleman et al. 1966; Wilkerson 1985; Gordon 2001). James Comer asserts this position more forcefully in *Waiting for a Miracle: Why Our Schools Cannot Solve Our Problems and How We Can* (1997). Colloquial knowledge among many parents "in the know" reflects awareness that there are a number of experiences and activities that occur outside of school that appear to enable schooling to work. In 1966, James Coleman concluded that differences in the family backgrounds of students, as opposed to school characteristics, accounted for the greatest amount of variance in their academic achievement. This finding was later found to be less so for low income and ethnic minority children than for the general population (Gordon 1999), but typically, family background and income stand as strong predictors of achievement in school. (Sexton 1961; Gordon and Meroe 1999; Jaynes and Williams 1989). In related works, Mercer (1973) and Wolf (1966, 1995) posited that it is the presence of family environmental supports for academic development that may explain this association between family status and student achievement. They made the now obvious point that books, positive models, help with homework, and a place to study in the home are associated with school achievement.

Racial and ethnic prejudice and discrimination continue to affect minority high achievement in a number of ways. The first is the lower academic expectations African American, Latino, and Native American students frequently encounter. The second is the damaging affect of ingrained stereotypes (which inaccurately posit that minority students are less intelligent than European or Asian students for genetic or cultural reasons) on minority students' "confidence and performance in demanding academic situations" (The College Board 1999). Thirdly, it is not inconceivable that some minority students deliberately minimize their academic efforts "out of a belief that success in school is only for white or Asian students" (The College Board 1999), or that their performance may serve to confirm existing stereotypes.

In addition to these sources of achievement disparities, both school-related and family-and community-related cultural differences contribute to the achievement gaps among minority and majority groups. School-related differences might involve a curriculum that does not effectively draw on students' cultural experiences (The College Board 1999). Similarly, family and community differences speak to the disquieting lack of economic and academic resources that families and communities need to facilitate their children's academic development. Unlike most disadvantaged parents and communities, academically successful parents and communities draw on their personal resources to provide a broad range of activities and supports designed to supplement their children's education. Taken together, these sources of academic disparities continue to produce, on a number of levels, the ubiquitous under-representation of minorities among top academic achieving students.

Superimposed on these population-specific factors are a broader set of issues that have to do with the changing nature of what it means to be an educated person in twenty-first century America. We live in a period marked by "urbanicity" and post-modernity.

Urbanicity refers to the continuous and greater concentration of people in specific geographic areas throughout human history. This trend can be traced from the episodic team efforts at hunting and other food-gathering activities of early humans; to the emergence of family, clan, and tribal kinship relationships—all efforts directed at mutual protection, food gathering, food cultivation, and territorial establishment; and to the control and enslavement practiced by feudal lords and slaveholders. It was evident in the concentrations of population made necessary by the Industrial Revolution, and was reflected in the organized systems of control practiced by the lords of capitalism, and even more recently, by the lords of socialism. It continues today in the spread of cultural and ideological systems facilitated by modern technology and economic exchange, sometimes called globalization.

Post-modernity is marked by ready access to the richness of resources and stimulation; diversity and pluralism of choice and expression; the declining stability of structures and values; ubiquitous discontinuities; and uncontrolled potential for de-stabilization and destruction. This juxtaposition of challenge and opportunity, of capacity and constraint, of fluidity and fixity, and of universality and idiosyncrasy—when superimposed on the circumstances of living in a national urban state where race matters—is what makes Education in Black America so problematic.

How might the nation approach this problem?

Toward the Improvement of the State of Education in Black America

Clearly the State of Education in Black America is multi-dimensional and complex. Arguably, the most critical problem in education that faces Black America is the problem of the gap in academic achievement known to exist between blacks and whites. While this problem is manifested at all achievement and socio-economic status (SES) levels, academic achievement disparities actually increase between high achieving minority and majority students. That is, the gap is smaller between low-achieving black and white students than it is between high-achieving students. The achievement gap is greater between back and white students from middle-class families than between black and white students from lower class families. In the aggregate, black students for whom at least one parent has a college degree tend to have SAT scores comparable to white students who have parents who have graduated from high school (Miller 1995). Obviously, this society has not been able to make education function to optimize and equalize academic development among blacks. This failure is not unique to the U.S.A. According to Ogbu (1978), in other industrialized societies in which caste-like systems are in place, we see comparable differentials in the academic achievement of high status and lower status children. There certainly appears to be a ubiquitous association between one's status in the social order and one's level of academic achievement that favors high status and privilege.

There are several possible explanations for this widely observed phenomenon that is reflected in the academic achievement gap. The most popular explanations rest with varying degrees of emphasis on assumed cultural and/or genetic differences between blacks and whites when race or ethnicity is the salient factor. In this line of argument, assumed inferiority is the underlying argument, whether it be genetically or culturally determined (Herrnstein and Murray 1994; Jensen 1969; Lewis 1966; and Shockley 1972). The most liberal scholars argue for cultural and behavioral differences that are not necessarily inferior but are, nonetheless, inappropriate to the demands of high levels of academic achievement, and these differences tend not to be addressed by typical approaches to schooling (Riessman 1962). Other more sophisticated explanations have focused on the attitudes and behaviors of the students themselves. Here we have the Fordham and Ogbu (1986) finding of "fear of acting white" as a factor that directs the attention and behavior of black students away from serious academic pursuit. More recently, Steele (1997) has advanced the notion concerning "fear of stereotype confirmation" in which black students' performance is assumed to be impaired by their anxiety concerning the possibility that if they try and do not do well they will confirm the negative stereotype that others hold concerning them. From the black community and other reasonably well-informed sources, we hear the argument that the achievement gap is a reflection of inadequate opportunities to learn. This argument rests on the historic finding of inequality in the educational opportunities available to children in the USA (Clark 1965; Coleman et al. 1966; Jaynes and William 1989; Kozol 1991; Miller 1995; Piven and Cloward 1971; and Sexton 1961). It is the inequality in educational opportunity that has been the driving force behind the school desegregation movement, and much of the continuing effort at school reform.

If that inequality in opportunity to learn and the inequality in achievement are ultimately to be eliminated, we think that it will be necessary that the nation undertake a multifaceted and differentiated initiative to improve the State of Education in Black America. We propose a tripartite program of interventions directed at:

- Reducing the hemorrhaging of potential and underdeveloped intellect in Black America, as is evidenced by the existence of the achievement gap and the relatively high levels of academic under-productivity observed in many of our children and the schools that serve them;

- Reducing inefficiencies in and the under-utilization of the power of schooling and supplemental education in the development of the sizeable group of children of color who now achieve at modest levels or barely survive with minimum performance in many of our schools; and

- Increasing the nurturance and celebration of developed ability in the group that Du Bois has called "the talented tenth" of our people upon whom the black community and the nation must depend for leadership.

In recent years Price (2002), the College Board (1999) and the Urban League have advocated that greater attention be given to high academic achievement in minority students. Gordon (1999; 2001; 2002) has been promoting the idea of a national effort at the "Affirmative Development of Academic Ability." This notion was first advanced at a conference sponsored by the National Action Committee on Minorities in Engineering, some twenty years ago. In an exchange with Scott Miller (1995) Gordon proposed that for affirmative action to work in a society where opportunities to learn are unequally distributed, it may be necessary that there be a parallel program directed at the affirmative development of academic ability. The notion was picked up a decade later in the recommendations of the College Board's National Task Force on Minority High Achievement (1999). "Thus, the Task Force recommends that an extensive array of public and private policies, actions, and investments be pursued, which would collectively provide many more opportunities for academic development for underrepresented minority students through the schools, colleges and universities that they attend, through their homes, and through their communities. I summarize this as a commitment to affirmative development."

In this line of argument, Gordon has elaborated Bourdieu's (1986) forms of capital to emphasize those capitals upon which effective education rests. These forms of capital include:

KINDS OF CAPITAL	DEFINITIONS
Health	physical developmental integrity, health, nutritional condition
Financial	income, wealth, family, community, and societal economic resources available for education

KINDS OF CAPITAL	DEFINITIONS (cont'd)
Human	social competence, tacit knowledge, and other education—derived abilities as personal or family assets
Social	social network relationships, social norms, cultural styles and values
Polity	societal membership, social concern, public commitment, political economy
Personal	disposition, attitudes, aspirations, efficacy, sense of power
Institutional	quality of and access to educational and socializing institutions
Pedagogical	supports for appropriate educational treatment in family, school, and community

Access to these forms of capital is grossly unequally distributed. Schools and other social institutions seem to work when the persons served bring to them the varieties of capital that enable and support human development. "Polity Capital," for example, refers to the reciprocal concern and respect, communal commitment, welcomed participation, and group affinity and inclusiveness that are associated with the sense of being a member of the society. The slogan for a major financial service corporation is "membership has its privileges." Polity refers to sense of membership. If I sense that I belong to the group, I tend to identify with the goals and values of the group. If I sense that I do not belong, then the values, standards and expectations of the group are less important and more easily ignored. If society recognizes me as a member, it is more like-ly to be concerned about my welfare and more willing to support the needs of other members who are like me. For example, if the people who use the public schools are "like me," it seems easier to raise tax-levied funds to support those schools. If the schools serve "those unlike me," public school budgets are likely to suffer. Societies and other human groups tend to emerge to meet the needs of those who are thought to belong or share polity.

Of all the human resource development capitals, polity capital may be the most important, since having it signals collective responsibility for my welfare. Thus, if we are correct in assuming that the effectiveness of schools and other human resource development institutions is in part a function of the availability of such wealth-derived capital for investment in human development, we may have in this relationship a catalyst for pedagogical, political, and social intervention.

If the effectiveness of education rests on such resources and they are unequally distributed, it is reasonable to anticipate that the effects of education will be unequal. The achievement distribution data correlate highly with the data on access to these forms of capital. My notion of affirmative development is conceptually grounded in possible approaches to offsetting the negative effects of the mal-distribution of access to these forms of education-related capital. While the most direct approach to the solution of the problem of mal-distribution would involve the re-distribution of income, wealth and related resources, it is not reasonable to expect that twenty-first century America would respond positively to such a radical solution. It is possible, however, that even a "compassionately conservative" society could consider it in the best interest of the nation to reorganize it's social institutions and their services in order to remove the negative effects of such mal-distribution on the academic and personal development of its people.

Affirmative Action

Until recently, our society has accepted the assignment of preferential treatment to designated categories of persons as special rewards for service to the nation, as compensation for unusual prior disadvantage, or simply as the entitlement associated with one's status. These various forms of affirmative action are currently under increased attack largely because of their public and colloquial association with minority group membership privilege. In all candor, affirmative action is also under attack because of abuses in its practice. Instead of an effort to ensure that qualified persons are not disqualified because of ethnicity and gender, affirmative action is often perceived as a program to privilege "unqualified" persons over those who are "qualified." The preoccupation with race may be a part of the problem. In a racist society all social arrangements are designed to reflect racist values. Explicit efforts to subvert those values are bound to come up against open resistance.

I propose a few adjustments. Rather than targeting ethnic or gender groups for affirmative action, I propose targeting larger and more diverse groups: those that are low on wealth and wealth-derived capital resources. Education and employment opportunities could be regarded as instruments of human resource development rather than agencies for the credentialing and rewarding of the "ablest." Rather than only protecting the opportunity to enter, let us also ensure the opportunity to develop and qualify. In addition to programs of affirmative action, which we vigorously support, we are proposing active programs of affirmative development.

A national effort at affirmative development to complement continuing efforts at affirmative action should be much broader than the initiatives directed at improving the effectiveness of education. Within the education establishment, however, we know a great deal about the deliberate development of academic ability. I propose that the education community embark upon a deliberate effort to develop academic abilities in a broad range of students who have a history of being deprived of resources and who as a consequence are underrepresented in the pool of academically high achieving students. The deliberate or affirmative development of academic ability should include more equitable access to the variety of capitals referred to above and to such educational interventions as:

• Early, continuous and progressive exposure to rigorous
  pre-academic and academic teaching and learning transactions.
  This should begin with high levels of language, literacy, and
  numeracy development.

- Rich opportunities to learn through pedagogical practices traditionally thought to be of excellent quality. We do not need to wait for new inventions: Benjamin Bloom's Mastery Learning, Robert Slavin's Success for All, James Comer's School Development, Bob Moses' Algebra Project, Vinetta Jones' Equity 2000; the College Board's Pacesetter, and Lauren Resnick's "effort-based" "thinking curriculum" all attempt to do some of this.

- Diagnostic, customized, and targeted assessment, instructional and remedial interventions.

- Academic acceleration-the increasing or speeding up of the pace of instruction and the enriching of the subject content rather than remediation.

- Using the relationships between different levels of student and program data to inform decisions concerning policies and practice.

- Making explicit what is to be learned and the processes by which they can be learned.

- Exposure to learning situations where academic excellence is expected.

- Helping students to understand how their minds work and can be used to further learning.

- Encouraging students to learn together.

- Special attention to the differential requirements of learning in different academic domains.

- Teaching students specific learning behaviors that are shown to improve academic achievement.

- Devoting special attention to the roles attitude, disposition, confidence, and efficacy play in success in learning.

- Access to a wide range of supplementary educational experiences—that variety of educational and developmental experiences that occur outside of and after school to ensure that schooling does in fact work, and that personal development is facilitated.

- The politicalization of academic learning in the lives of members of groups that have been subordinated by mainstream culture yet have developed alternative strategies of resistance to the mainstream culture.

The state of education in Black America is considerably better than it was 100 years ago—better than even 50 years ago. However, evidence suggests that our progress has been uneven during the past fifty years. There is no doubt that we face complex and serious problems related to the significant gap between the academic achievement levels of peoples of color and the achievement levels of Asian American and European American peoples. But even more problematic may be the changing and rising demands for intellectual competence at the same time that black people are trying to close the academic achievement gap. Such a moving target may in fact exacerbate the challenge. That possibility underscores the need for a national commitment to the affirmative development of academic ability in black and other populations that are under-represented among the achievers in our society.

Professor Gordon acknowledges with deep appreciation the assistance of Beatrice L. Bridglall and Brenda X. Mejia in the development of this paper, and financial support from the Rockefeller Foundation and The College Board.

References

American Council on Education. 2003. *Minorities in higher education 2002-2003., Twentieth annual status report.* Washington, DC: Author.

American Council on Education 2000. *Minorities in higher education 1999-2000. Sixteenth annual status report.* Washington, DC: Author.

Bourdieu, P. 1986. The forms of capital. In J. Richardson (Ed.), *Handbook of theory and research for the sociology of education* (pp. 241–258). Westport, CT: Greenwood.

Clark, K. 1965. *Dark guetto.* New York: Harper & Row.

Coleman, J.S., Campbell, E.Q., Hobson, C.J., McPartland, J., Mood, A.M., Weinfield, F.D., et al. 1966. *Equality of educational opportunity.* Washington, DC: U.S. Government Printing Office.

Comer, J. 1997. *Waiting for a miracle: Why our schools can't solve our problems—and how we can.* New York: Dutton.

The College Board. 1999. *Reaching the top: A report of the National Task Force on Minority High Achievement.* New York: Author.

Gordon, E.W. (Ed.). 1999. *Education and justice: A view from the back of the bus.* New York: Teachers College Press.

Gordon, E.W. 2001. Affirmative Development of Academic Ability. *Pedagogical Inquiry and Praxis,* 2. Gordon, E.W. & Bridglall, B.L (Eds.). Institute for Urban and Minority Education, Teachers College, Columbia University & The College Board, NY.

Gordon, E.W. 2002. Affirmative development: Looking beyond racial inequality. *College Board Review,* 195, 28–33.

Gordon, E.W. and A.S. Meroe, 1999. Common destinies–Continuing dilemmas. In E. W. Gordon, *Education and justice: A view from back of the bus.* New York: Teachers College Press.

Herrnstein, R. J., and C. Murray, 1994. *The bell curve: Intelligence and class structure in American life*. New York: The Free Press.

Hoffman, K., Lieges, C. and Snyder, T. 2003. *Status and trends in the education of blacks*. Washington, D.C.: National Center for Education Statistics.

Jaynes, G.D., and R. M. William (Eds.). 1989. *Common destiny*. Washington, D.C.: National Academy Press.

Jensen, A. R. 1969. How much can we boost IQ and scholastic achievement? *Harvard Educational Review*, 39, 1–23.

Kozol, J. 1991. *Savage inequalities: Children in America's schools*. New York, NY: Crown Publishers.

Lewis, O. 1966. *A Puerto Rican family in the culture of poverty*. New York: Random House.

Mercer, J.R. 1973. *Labeling the mentally retarded: Clinical and social system perspectives on mental retardation*. Berkeley: University of California Press.

Miller, L.S. 1995. *An American imperative: Accelerating minority educational advancement*. New Haven, CT: Yale University Press.

Ogbu, J. 1978. *Minority education and caste: the American system in cross-cultural perspective*. New York: Academic Press.

Piven, F. F., and R. A. Cloward. 1971. *Regulating the poor: The functions of public welfare*. New York: Pantheon Books.

Price, H. 2002. *Achievement matters: Getting your child the best education possible*. New York: Kensington Publishing Corporation.

Riessman, F. 1962. *The culturally deprived child*. New York: Harper and Row.

Sexton, V. 1961. *Education and income: Inequalities of opportunity in our public schools*. New York: Viking Press.

Shockley, W. 1972. Dysgenics, geneticity, raceology: A challenge to
the intellectual responsibility of educators. *Phi Delta Kappan*, 53(5), 297-307.

Steele, C. M. 1997. A threat in the air: How stereotypes shape
intellectual identity and performance. *American Psychologist*, 52(6), 613–629.

Wilkerson, D.A. 1985. *Educating all our children.* Westport, CT: Mediax.

Wolf, R.M. 1966. The measurement of environments. In A. Anastasi
(Ed.), *Testing problems in perspective* (pp. 491-503). Washington, D.C.: American
Council in Education.

Wolf, R.M. 1995. The measurement of environments: a follow-up study. *The Journal
of Negro Education*, 64(3), 354-59.

Health and the Quality of Life Among African Americans

By David R. Williams

In 1999, a national study revealed that most Americans were unaware that racial disparities in health exist (Kaiser Family Foundation, 1999). Strikingly, 54 percent of whites, 58 percent of African Americans, and 65 percent of Hispanics were unaware that black infants have a higher death rate than white infants. Similarly, 57 percent of whites, 53 percent of African Americans, and 68 percent of Hispanics did not know that the average black adult has a shorter life expectancy than the average white person. Effectively mobilizing support to address racial disparities in health is contingent on a broad recognition that a problem exists. This chapter seeks to provide an overview of racial disparities in health by describing 10 key facts relevant to understanding African American health. A word about terminology: the population of African descent in the U.S. is divided over preferred racial terminology, with 44 percent preferring the term "black" and 28 percent preferring "African American" (Tucker et al. 1996). In an effort to recognize individual dignity, I use these two terms interchangeably.

KEY FACT#1: Racial differences in health exist for many health conditions.

Higher rates of illness and death for African Americans compared to whites exist for a broad range of health outcomes. Table 1 shows the top 15 causes of death (mortality) in the U.S. in 2001 and the number of deaths and the black-white ratio for each condition. A ratio greater than 1.0 means that blacks have higher mortality than whites. A ratio less than 1.0 indicates that the black rate is lower than that of whites. The overall death

TABLE 1

Racial Differences in Death Rates, 2001
15 Leading Causes of Death in the U.S.

Rank	Cause of Death	Number of Deaths	Black/White Death Rates[1]
--	All Causes	2,416,425	1.3
1.	Heart Disease	700,142	1.3
2.	Cancer	553,768	1.3
3.	Stroke	163,538	1.4
4.	Respiratory Diseases	123,013	0.7
5.	Accidents	101,537	1.0
6.	Diabetes	71,372	2.1
7.	Flu and Pneumonia	62,034	1.1
8.	Alzheimer's Disease	53,852	0.7
9.	Kidney Disease	39,480	2.4
10.	Septicemia	32,238	2.3
11.	Suicide	30,622	0.5
12.	Liver Disease and Cirrhosis	27,035	1.0
13.	Homicide	20,308	4.3
14.	Hypertension	19,250	2.9
15.	Inflammation of the Lungs	17,301	1.1

Source: National Vital Statistics Reports, (Arias et al. 2003); [1] Age-adjusted death rates per 100,000 population

rate for African Americans is 30 percent higher than that of whites. A similar pattern can be seen for most diseases with blacks having higher mortality than whites for 10 of the 15 leading causes of death. African American death rates are at least twice as high as those of whites for diabetes, kidney disease, septicemia, homicide and hypertension. The rates are equivalent for accidents and liver cirrhosis and lower for blacks than whites for suicide, chronic lower respiratory diseases and Alzheimer's disease.

KEY FACT #2: In the last 50 years, although overall health has improved, racial differences in health are unchanged or have widened.

During the last half-century, the U.S. has witnessed an expansion in access to health care, marked increases in medical research, knowledge, and technology and numerous initiatives to improve social and economic opportunities for the disadvantaged. Table 2 shows overall and infant mortality rates for blacks and whites from 1950 to 2000. There is good news and bad news in these data. The good news is that the health of both blacks and whites has improved over time. The overall death rates for whites were 40 percent lower in 2000 than in 1950. For African Americans, the decline was 35 percent. For both racial groups, the decline in the infant mortality (the death of a baby before his or her first birthday) is even more dramatic. However, although there has been some reduction in the absolute racial differences in mortality, there has been no progress in reducing the relative difference in health between blacks and whites. The age-adjusted overall death rate for African Americans was 20 percent higher than that of whites in 1950 but 30 percent higher in 2000. Similarly, a black baby born in the U.S.A. was 1.6 times as likely to die before his/her first birthday than a white infant in 1950, but is 2.5 times as likely in 2000.

To translate these dry statistics into a meaningful unit of analysis, a 1985 government report used the concept of "excess deaths" (DHHS, 1985). Excess deaths refers to the number of African Americans who die each year who would not die if the black population had a mortality rate that was the same as that of the whites. Table 3 presents data from a recent

TABLE 2

All-Cause Mortality Rates and Infant Mortality Rates, 1950-2000

Mortality- All Causes [1]				Infant Mortality [2]		
Year	White (W)	Black (B)	B/W Ratio	White (W)	Black (B)	B/W Ratio
1950	14.1	17.2	1.2	26.8	43.9	1.6
1960	13.1	15.8	1.2	22.9	44.3	1.9
1970	11.9	15.2	1.3	17.8	32.6	1.8
1980	10.1	13.1	1.3	10.9	22.2	2.0
1990	9.1	12.5	1.4	7.6	18.0	2.4
2000	8.5	11.2	1.3	5.7	14.1	2.5

Source: National Center for Health Statistics, 2003
[1]Age-adjusted, per 1,000 population   [2] Deaths per 1,000 live births

study that has calculated the number of excess deaths from 1940 to 1999 (Levine et al. 2001) The annual number of premature deaths for blacks has increased from 66,900 in 1940 (183 per day) to 96,800 in 1998 (265 per day). This report estimated that the total number of excess deaths for African Americans was an incredible 4.3 million between 1940 and 1999. Thus, the elevated death rates for African Americans is a major national tragedy that reflects the loss of hundreds of American lives each day during their most economically productive years. It begs for a comprehensive national response that would arrest the loss of so many lives each year.

TABLE 3

Excess Deaths[1] for Black Population

Year	Avg. No./Day	Avg. No./Year
1940	183	66,900
1950	144	52,700
1960	139	50,900
1970	198	72,200
1980	221	80,600
1990	285	103,900
1998	265	96,800

TOTAL Premature Deaths, 1940-1999 = 4,272,000

Source: National Center for Health Statistics data, (Levine, et al. 2001)
[1]Excess deaths= number of deaths in the black population that would not occur if the death rates of African Americans was equivalent to those of whites.

KEY FACT #3: Socioeconomic Status (SES) is a central but incomplete explanation of racial differences in health.

Early studies of racial differences in health attributed them to biological differences between blacks and whites. Scientific research indicates that our racial categories do not do a good job of capturing genetic variation (American Association of Physical Anthropology, 1996). Small genetic differences between racial groups can interact with environmental factors to affect health, but since race is more of a social category than a biological one, genetic explanations are unlikely to play a major role in explaining the observed racial disparities in health. Race is nonetheless consequential as a social factor with African Americans having lower levels of income, education, occupational status, and wealth, and higher rates of poverty and unemployment than whites. These socioeconomic status (SES) indicators are some of the strongest known determinants of variations in health and account for a large part of the racial differences in disease (Williams and Collins, 1995).

Table 4 presents national data on life expectancy at age 45 by years of education to illustrate the association between race, SES and health. First, Table 4 shows that at age 45, white men and women can expect to live a nontrivial 3.2 years longer than their black counterparts. Second, racial differences in life expectancy become smaller when blacks and whites are compared at similar levels of education. At the same time, striking racial differences in life expectancy persist at every level of education. For example, if we compare blacks and whites who have not graduated from high school, white males live 2.6 years longer, and white

TABLE 4

Life Expectancy at Age 45 for Blacks and Whites

Education	MALES			FEMALES		
	White	Black	**RACE DIFF.**	White	Black	**RACE DIFF.**
All	31.4	28.2	**3.2**	37.4	34.2	**3.2**
0-11 yrs	29.6	27.0	**2.6**	36.1	32.9	**3.2**
12 yrs	31.6	29.2	**2.4**	37.9	35.1	**2.8**
13+ yrs	33.6	31.7	**1.9**	38.6	37.5	**1.1**
Educ. Diff.	**4.0**	**4.7**		**2.5**	**4.6**	

Source: National Longitudinal Mortality Study, 1979-1989, (Lin et al., 2003)

women 3.2 years longer than black counterparts. At the highest education level in the table, white men and women at age 45 outlive their black peers by 1.9 years and 1.1 years, respectively.

Third, the differences in life expectancy by education, within each race and gender group (with the exception of white women), are larger than the racial differences. For example, white men in the highest education group can expect to live 4 years longer at age 45 than white men in the lowest education group. The comparable difference for black men is 4.7 years. Similarly, white females with 0-11 years of education have a life expectancy that is 2.5 years shorter than those with 13 or more years. Among African-American women, the life expectancy difference between the lowest and highest education group is 4.6 years. A similar pattern of larger health status differences by SES than by race has been found for other health outcomes. These data clearly indicate that although economic circumstances are central to racial differences in health, there are other factors linked to race that are also having an impact.

TABLE 5

Black-White Differences in Infant Mortality[1] by Mother's Education: U.S. Women, 20 years of age and older, 1995

Maternal Education	White	Black	Black/White Ratio
<12 years	9.9	17.3	1.74
12 years	6.5	14.8	2.28
13-15 years	5.1	12.3	2.41
≥ 16 years	4.2	11.4	2.71

Source: National Center for Health Statistics, (Pamuk et al., 1998).
[1]Deaths per 1,000 live births

This point is dramatically illustrated in Table 5 with national infant mortality data. Four points are noteworthy. First, for both black and white women, increasing years of education is associated with lower levels of infant mortality. Second, there is a striking racial difference at every level of education. Third, surprisingly, the black/white ratios become larger as education increases. Compared to similarly educated white females, infants born to black women who have not completed high school are 1.7 times more likely to die before their first birthday, and those born to black college graduates have an infant death rate that is 2.7 times greater. Fourth, the most disadvantaged white group (women who have not com-

TABLE 6

Median Income in 2000 by Education for Full-Time Workers 25 years of age and over, U.S.

	MALES		FEMALES	
Education	White	Black	White	Black
9th-11th grade	25,030	21,527	16,957	17,849
High School Graduate	34,583	27,454	24,579	21,081
Some College	40,028	35,512	27,401	26,293
Associate Degree	41,864	31,512	30,567	27,131
Bachelor's Degree	55,270	45,068	38,509	38,017
Master's Degree	65,101	50,630	47,142	45,076
Professional Degree	94,709	62,462	56,405	67,088
Doctorate	76,312	73,614	55,581	54,289

Source: Bureau of Labor Statistics and Bureau of the Census, (Current Population Survey, 2001)

pleted high school) has a lower infant mortality rate than the most advantaged black group (college graduates).

KEY FACT #4: All indicators of SES are not equivalent across racial groups.
The persistence of racial differences in health after SES is controlled reflects, in part, that a given level of income, education and occupation are not truly comparable across race (Williams and Collins, 1995). There are large racial differences in the quality of elementary and high school education, such that black high school graduates bring fewer basic skills to the labor market than their white counterparts. In addition, as Table 6 shows, at every level of education whites have higher individual earnings than blacks. These differences are larger among males than among females (and are sometimes non-existent or even reversed for women). However, because white women are more likely to be married than black women, other data reveal that at every level of education, black women reside in households that earn markedly less family income than whites. There are also racial differences in the purchasing power of income, because blacks tend to reside in areas where the costs of a broad range of goods and services including food and housing are higher than those of whites. Middle-class blacks are also more likely to experience unemployment than their white peers and employed blacks are more likely than their white counterparts to be exposed to occupational hazards and carcinogens, even after adjusting for job experience and education (Williams and Collins, 1995).

Moreover, there are large racial differences in the inheritance of wealth so that racial differences in wealth are much larger than those for income. Table 7 shows that the median net worth (wealth) of whites is almost 7 times that of blacks and Hispanics. Moreover, at every level of income, blacks and Hispanics have considerably less wealth than their white peers so that racial differences in income understate the racial gap in economic resources. Racial differences in wealth also link the current situation of blacks to historic discrimination. For most American families, housing equity is a major source of wealth. Thus, today's black-white differences in wealth are, at least partly, a consequence of the institutional discrimi-

TABLE 7

Median Net Worth by Race and Household Income, 1995

Household Income	White	Black	Hispanic
Total	$49,030	$7,073	$7,255
Poorest 20%	$9,720	$1,500	$1,250
2nd Quintile	$26,534	$3,998	$3,898
3rd Quintile	$42,123	$11,623	$10,377
4th Quintile	$57,445	$27,275	$19,424
Richest 20%	$123,781	$40,866	$80,416

Source: U.S. Census Bureau, Survey of Income and Program Participation, (Davern et al. 2001)

nation in housing practiced in the past (Oliver and Shapiro, 1997). Research in the health field indicates that higher levels of wealth are associated with better health.

KEY FACT #5: Racism is an added burden that adversely affects African-American health.

Another reason for racial differences in health even at 'equivalent' levels of SES is the added contribution of racism to health (Williams and Collins 1995). A growing body of research indicates that racism adversely affects the health of African Americans through multiple mechanisms. First, and most importantly, residential segregation, an institutional mechanism of racism, can affect health by creating racial differences in residential environments, educational and employment opportunities, SES, and access to goods and services (Williams and Collins 2003). For example, an analysis of the effects of segregation on young African Americans making the transition from school to work found that the elimination of residential segregation would completely erase black-white differences in earnings, high school graduation rates, and unemployment and would reduce racial differences in single motherhood by two-thirds (Cutler et al. 1997).

High levels of segregation also create distinctive residential environments for African Americans. Sampson and Wilson (1995) report that in the 171 largest cities in the U.S., there was not even one where whites lived in comparable conditions to blacks in terms of poverty rates or rates of single parent households. These researchers concluded that "the worst urban context in which whites reside is considerably better than the average context of black communities." These conditions created by poverty and segregation make it more difficult for residents of those areas to practice desirable health behaviors. The higher cost and poorer quality of grocery items in economically disadvantaged neighborhoods can lead to poorer nutrition. The tobacco and alcohol industry heavily target poor minority communities with advertising for their products. The absence of recreation facilities and concerns about personal safety can discourage participation in regular exercise. Moreover, the concentration of poverty can lead to exposure to elevated levels of economic hardship, as well as other types of chronic and acute stressors. For example, African Americans are much more likely than whites to be victims of all types of violent crime. The weakened community and neighborhood infrastructure in segregated areas can also adversely affect interpersonal relationships and trust among neighbors. Finally, poor, segregated communities often have unequal access to a broad range of services because of municipal neglect and disinvestment. The resulting decline in the urban infrastructure and physical environment can result in disproportionate exposure to environmental toxins and poor quality housing.

Second, the subjective experience of discrimination is a neglected but important source of stress. Research indicates that acute and chronic experiences of discrimination are stressful incidents that are adversely related to physical and mental health and can make an incremental contribution, above SES, to accounting for racial differences in health (Williams et al. 2003). Third, a small but growing body of research indicates the health of African Americans is adversely affected when they buy into the larger society's negative characterization of blacks.

KEY FACT #6: There are racial differences in access to care.

Access to medical care is a significant challenge for many African Americans. Table 8 shows that compared to whites, African Americans have lower levels of private insurance coverage, higher rates of public insurance (Medicaid), and higher rates of being without any insurance. Blacks are also more likely than whites to receive care in non-optimal organizational settings (such as the emergency room) and to lack continuity in the health care received. A high proportion of both black and white adults have inadequate access to dental care with 24 percent of whites aged 18 to 64 and 48 percent of similarly aged African Americans having untreated dental caries. Thus, although African Americans have greater need for medical care due to higher levels of illness, they are more likely than whites to face multiple barriers in accessing health care services.

TABLE 8

Race and Access to Care, 2001

Indicator	White	Black
1. Private insurance [1]	79%	58%
2. Medicaid (public, means tested) [1]	7%	20%
3. No health insurance [1]	12%	19%
4. No health care visit, past year	14%	16%
5. No usual source of care [2]	14%	17%
6. No dental visit, past year [2]	30%	43%
7. Untreated dental caries, [2] 1988-94	24%	48%

Source: National Center for Health Statistics 2003, [1] Under Age 65, [2] Ages 18-64

KEY FACT #7: There are racial differences in the quality of care.

There are also systematic racial differences in the receipt of a broad spectrum of therapeutic interventions. A recent Institute of Medicine (IOM) report entitled "Unequal Treatment" documents large racial/ethnic differences in the quality and intensity of medical care in the United States (Smedley et al. 2003). For virtually every type of therapeutic procedure, ranging from high technology interventions to the most basic diagnostic and treatment procedures, blacks and other minorities are less likely to receive medical procedures and to experience poorer quality medical care than whites. This pattern of poorer quality and less intensive care persists even in studies that adjust for differences in health insurance, SES, stage and severity of disease, comorbidity, and the type of medical facility. These disparities in care also exist in contexts such as Veterans Administration Health system (VA) and among Medicare inpatients where differences in insurance factors are minimized.

The IOM report concluded that multiple factors contribute to these disparities in care. They include the geographic mal-distribution of health resources, policies and procedures of larger health systems and both patient and provider behavior. However, the report also concluded that discrimination by providers contributes to racial/ethnic disparities in care. Much of this bias is likely to be unconscious or unthinking discrimination based on negative stereotypes. Research on stereotypes indicates that when an individual who holds a negative stereotype about a group and meets someone who fits the stereotype s/he will discriminate against that individual (Smedley et al. 2003). Strikingly, stereotype-linked bias is both an automatic process and an unconscious one, even among persons who are not prejudiced.

Several lines of evidence suggest that discrimination based on negative stereotypes of minorities is likely to play a role in encounters between patients and providers in the U.S. First, health care providers are a part of the larger society that views blacks and other minorities negatively. For example, national data reveal that whites view blacks, Hispanics and Asians more negatively than they view themselves with perceptions of blacks being the most unfavorable and with Hispanics being viewed twice as negatively as Asians (Williams 2001). For example, 44 percent of whites believe that blacks are lazy, 51 percent that blacks are prone to violence and 56 percent that blacks prefer to live off welfare. Comparatively, 5 percent of whites view whites as lazy, 16 percent view them as prone to violence, and 4 percent as preferring to live off welfare. Second, research on stereotypes indicates that they are more likely to be activated under conditions of time pressure, the need to make quick judgments, cognitive overload and task complexity. The typical health care encounter often contains these characteristics. Third, a few studies have found that physicians perceive black patients more negatively than their white counterparts.

KEY FACT #8: African Americans are still under-represented among health professionals.

There has been only a relatively small increase in the proportion of African-American physicians in medicine in the last 30 years. Black physicians increased from 2.5 percent of all U.S. physicians prior to 1968 (Carlisle et al. 1998) to 2.9 percent currently (Lancet Editorial 1999). Table 9 shows the enrollment of blacks, other racial groups and women in medical schools for 1970 and 2000. Blacks increased from 4.5 percent to 4.7 percent of dental school enrollees and from 3.8 percent to 7.4 percent of those in medical school. Hispanics and American Indians are also underrepresented in medical and dental schools while there have been dramatic increases in the enrollment of women and of Asians. Research indicates that affirmative action programs (federal initiatives that allowed schools and employers to take into consideration a qualified applicant's race, sex, national origin or disability) have been successful. It is estimated that affirmative action is responsible for 40 percent of all U.S.-trained physicians from underrepresented minority backgrounds (Lancet Editorial 1999). Although underrepresented minority students tend to have lower test scores than other medical students, they do not differ on clinical performance, suggesting that other non-cognitive variables are essential in the recruitment of competent physicians (Tekian 1997). In addition, despite their current unpopularity, affirmative action programs are defensible on multiple grounds including the societal obligation to

TABLE 9

Enrollment in Medical and Dental Schools: Blacks, Other Races, Women

Professional School	1970-71	2000-01
Dentistry	Percentages	
Black	4.5	4.7
White	91.4	64.4
Hispanic	1.0	5.3
American Indian	0.1	0.6
Asian	2.6	25.0
All Women 1	3.1	37.6
Medicine (Allopathic)		
Black	3.8	7.4
White	94.3	63.8
Hispanic	0.5	6.4
American Indian	0.0	0.8
Asian	1.4	20.1
All Women 1	13.7	44.4

Source: National Center for Health Statistics, 2003; [1] Comparison years for women are 1971-72 with 1999-2000.

meet the health care needs of all segments of the population (Nickens and Jordan, 1996). Black and Hispanic physicians are much more likely than others to care for the uninsured and those with Medicaid and to practice in urban and rural under served areas (Komaromy et al., 1996). A recent study reported that in order to reach racial and ethnic population parity, the U.S. needs to double the number of black and Hispanic first-year residents and triple the number of Native American residents (Libby et al., 1997). White first-year residents would need to be reduced by two-fifths and Asians by two-thirds. Current trends do not suggest that these goals are likely to be reached.

KEY FACT #9: African Americans have much better mental health than expected.

It was noted in Table 1 that blacks have markedly lower rates of suicide than whites. The low level of suicide is consistent with other mental health data and reflects a well-documented paradox in the health literature. African Americans tend to have higher levels of ill health than whites for most indicators of physical health, but they have comparable or lower rates of mental illness than whites. The Epidemiologic Catchment Area Study (ECA), the largest study of psychiatric disorders

TABLE 10

Rates of Psychiatric Disorders and Black/White Ratios

Disorder Category	%	B/W Ratio
1. Any affective disorder	11.3	0.78
2. Any anxiety disorder	17.1	0.90
3. Any substance abuse/dependence	11.3	0.47
4. Any disorder	29.5	0.70

Source: National Comorbidity Study, (Kessler et al. 1994).

ever conducted in the United States found very few differences between blacks and whites in the rates of both current and lifetime psychiatric disorders. This study focused on persons in treatment, as well as those not in treatment. Especially striking was the absence of a racial difference in drug use history and the prevalence of alcohol and drug abuse dependence. Anxiety disorders, especially phobias, stand out as one area where blacks had considerably higher rates than whites.

Table 10 shows findings from the National Comorbidity Survey (NCS), the first study to use a national probability sample to assess psychiatric disorders in the United States (Kessler et al. 1994). The first column shows the overall rate for each major class of psychiatric disorders and the second column shows the black/white ratios for each major class of disorders. These data reveal that blacks do not have higher rates of disorder than whites for any of the major classes of disorders. Instead, lower rates of mental illness for blacks than whites are especially pronounced for the affective disorders (depression) and the substance abuse disorders (alcohol and drug abuse). These findings highlight the need to attend the resources and strengths of the African-American community that shields this population from at least some of the negative consequences of exposure to stressors. Much attention to black health has focused only on pathologies and deficits and given scant attention to the resources and cultural strengths within minority communities. High levels of religious involvement, family and kin support systems, psychological resources, and racial identity have all been identified as potential adaptive resources within the black population.

KEY FACT #10: Policies to reduce inequalities in health must address fundamental non-medical determinants.

Addressing disparities in health will require eliminating inequalities in healthcare access and quality. However, improved medical care alone is unlikely to eliminate racial inequalities in health. Medical care is an important but limited determinant of health. It is estimated that medical care explains only about 10 percent of the differences in adult health (U.S. Department of Health, Education, and Welfare 1979). Nonetheless, medical care may have a greater impact on the health status of vulnerable populations, such as African Americans than on the population in general. Healthcare may be an especially important health-protective resource in the context of multiple vulnerabilities. Thus, greater access to more continuous, preventive care and timely and appropriate secondary and tertiary care from concerned providers can reduce disparities in care and lead to improvements in health status (Politzer et al. 2001).

At the same time, improving overall health and reducing inequalities in health will require altering conditions in residential and working environments to maximize health enhancing activities and to buffer against negative exposures. Thus, larger societal policies have the potential to improve overall levels of health and reduce social inequalities in health. U.S. policy makers can learn from comprehensive national plans recently implemented by both the British (Department of Health 2003) and the Dutch (Mackenbach and Stronks 2002) to reduce socioeconomic and racial/ethnic inequalities in health. Both governments have allocated resources to enhance access to care and improve the quality of care for vulnerable groups. However, a striking feature of both the British and Dutch approaches to reducing health disparities is the emphasis given, appropriately, to the non-medical determinants of health. For example, British initiatives address broad areas such as income policy, education, housing, employment and nutritional policies. To improve health, programs have been implemented to enhance education, employment, housing, transportation and preschool opportunities.

Initiatives in the Netherlands are equally comprehensive. Proposed policies to reduce inequalities in health include enhancing educational achievement among low SES children, implementing new tax and income support policies to prevent an increase in income inequality, reducing long-term poverty through new programs that assist the chronically unemployed to find paid employment, and providing additional financial resources for very poor families with children. Other initiatives call for new health promotion programs targeted to low SES groups, that emphasize environmental measures, such as providing free fruit at elementary schools and increasing tobacco taxes to reduce consumption. Innovative strategies include using schools as sites for health promotion programs targeted at students from low SES families, incorporating health promotion into urban renewal programs and re-engineering work conditions to reduce the physical workload of manual jobs. Improving African-American health in the U.S. must build on the cornerstone of strengthening the physical infrastructure and enhancing the human capital of the populations in disadvantaged, segregated communities. It has been recently argued that reparations, targeted not at individuals but at enhancing social and economic development in African-American areas are one option for infusing the needed capital to improve the living conditions and health of the black population (Williams and Collins 2003).

Conclusion

This chapter has outlined the health challenges facing the African American population by making comparisons to the white population. However, the white population does not have ideal levels of health. Although the United States spends more per person on medical care and medical research than any other country in the world, Table 11 reveals that the world's only super power ranks 28th in the world on infant mortality, 24th on life expectancy at birth for men and 21st on life expectancy for women. This disappointing profile does not just reflect the poor health of blacks or other minorities. If the white population in the U.S. were a country, 23 countries in the world would have lower infant mortality rates, 19 would have lower life expectancy for men and 18 would have lower life expectancy for women. As a country, U.S. blacks would rank 36th in the world on infant mortality, 34th on life expectancy for men and 35th on life expectancy for women. In terms of both infant mortality and life expectancy, males and females born in Cuba enjoy better health than African Americans.

It is a national embarrassment that there are large and persisting racial differences in health. These inequities fly in the face of cherished American principles of equality. Although the problems linked to economic inequality disproportionately affect blacks in the United States, they also affect a large number of persons in the country more generally.

TABLE 11

International Comparisons in Infant Mortality and Life Expectancy

Rank	Infant Mortality, 1999 Deaths per 1,000 births	Life Expectancy at Birth, 1998 Men	Women
1	Hong Kong (3.1)	Hong Kong (77.4)	Japan (84.0)
2	Japan (3.4)	Japan (77.2)	Hong Kong (83.0)
3	Sweden (3.4)	Sweden (76.9)	France (82.4)
4	Singapore (3.5)	Switzerland (76.3)	Switzerland (82.4)
5	Finland (3.7)	Israel (76.2)	Italy (82.2)
6	Norway (3.9)	Canada (76.0)	Spain (82.2)
7	Denmark (4.2)	Australia (75.9)	Sweden (81.9)
8	France (4.3)	Italy (75.9)	Australia (81.5)
9	Austria (4.4)	Cuba (75.8)	Canada (81.5)
19	Ireland (5.5)	Austria (74.7)	U.S. WHITE (80.0)
20	New Zealand (5.5)	U.S. WHITE (74.5)	Northern Ireland (79.8)
21	Portugal (5.6)	Belgium (74.3)	**United States (79.5)**
24	U.S. WHITE (5.8)	**United States (73.8)**	Puerto Rico (79.3)
26	Cuba (6.4)	Finland (77.6)	Portugal (78.9)
28	**United States (7.1)**	Chile (72.3)	Chile (78.3)
33	Puerto Rico (10.6)	Slovakia (68.7)	Slovakia (77.0)
34	Costa Rica (11.8)	U.S. BLACK (67.6)	Hungary (75.2)
35	Bulgaria (14.5)	Bulgaria (67.4)	U.S. BLACK (74.8)
36	U.S. BLACK (14.6)	Romania (66.3)	Bulgaria (74.7)
37	Russian Federation (17.1)	Hungary (66.1)	Romania (73.8)

Source: National Center for Health Statistics 2003.

Two-thirds of all poor persons in the United States are white. The factors that determine the health of blacks are the same forces, on a less intensive scale, that affects the health of the entire population. That is, the health of black Americans can be viewed as the visible tip of an iceberg that reflects conditions that are increasing health risks throughout the population as a whole. Although intervention efforts must be must be sensitive to the tip of the iceberg, policies are needed that also serve to improve the average health of the entire population. Moreover, since disease causing agents know no color line, health problems eventually diffuse from pockets of disadvantage to the general population. Thus, it is in the best interest of the entire society to reduce the racial gap in SES and health. Investments to improve the social conditions and the health of African Americans can improve the health of the entire U.S. population and have long-term positive consequences for non-blacks as well.

References

American Association of Physical Anthropology. 1996. "AAPA statement on biological aspects of race." *American Journal of Physical Anthropology* 101:569-70.

Arias, Elizabeth, Robert N. Anderson, Kung Hsiang-Ching, Sherry L. Murphy, and Kenneth D. Kochanek. 2003. "Deaths: Final Data for 2001." *National Vital Statistics Reports, Centers for Disease Control and Prevention* 52: (3), September 18, 2003.

Current Population Survey. 2001. Annual Demographic Survey, March 2001. Table PINC - 03. Bureau of Labor Statistics and Bureau of the Census. http://ferret.bls.census.gov/macro/032002/perinc/new03_000. Accessed December 14, 2003.

Carlisle, David M. and Jill E. Liu Honghu Gardner. 1998. "The Entry of Underrepresented Minority Students Into US Medical Schools: An Evaluation of Recent Trends." *American Journal of Public Health* 88:1314-8.

Cutler D.M., E.L. Glaeser, and J.L. Vigdor. 1997. "Are ghettos good or bad?" *Quarterly Journal of Economics* 112:827-72.

Davern, Michael E. and Patricia J. Fisher. 2001. *U.S. Census Bureau, Current Population Reports, Household Economic Studies Series. Household Net Worth and Asset Ownership:* 1995. Washington, D.C.: U.S. Government Printing Office.

Department of Health. 2003. *Tackling Health Inequalities: A Programme for Action.* United Kingdom: Dept. of Health Publications, http://www.info.doh.gov.uk/doh/int-press.nsf/page/2003-0247.

Department of Health and Human Services. 1985. *Report of the secretary on black and minority health.* Washington, D.C.: U.S. Department of Health.

Kaiser, Henry J. Family Foundation. 1999. *Race, Ethnicity, and Medical Care: A Survey of Public Perceptions and Experiences.* Menlo Park, CA: Kaiser Foundation.

Kessler, Ronald C., Katherine A. McGonagle, Shanyang Zhao, Christopher B. Nelson, Michael Hughes, Suzanne Eshleman, Hans-Ulrich Wittchen, and Kenneth S. Kendler. 1994. "Lifetime and 12-month prevalence of DSM-III-R psychiatric disorders in the United States." *Archives of General Psychiatry* 51:8-19.

Komaromy, Miriam, Kevin Grumbach, Michael Drake, Karen Vranizan, Nicole Lurie, Dennis Keane, and Andrew Bindman. 1996. "The Role Of Black And Hispanic Physicians In Providing Health Care For Underserved Populations." *Black and Hispanic Physicians and Underserved Populations* 334:1305-10.

Lancet Editorial. 1999. "Affirmative Action." *The Lancet* 353:1.

Levine, Robert S., James E. Foster, Robert E. Fullilove, Nathaniel C. Briggs, Pamela C. Hull, Baqar A. Husaini, and Charles H. Hennekens. 2001. "Black-white inequalities in mortality and life expectancy, 1933-1999: implications for Health People 2010." *Public Health Reports* 116:474-83.

Libby, D. L., Z. Zhou, and D. A. Kindig. 1997. "Will minority physician supply meet U. S. needs?" *Health Affairs* 16:205-14.

Lin, Charles C., Eugene Rogot, Norman J. Johnson , Paul D. Sorlie, and Elizabeth Arias. 2003. "A further study of life expectancy by socioeconomic factors in the National Longitudinal Mortality." *Ethnicity and Disease* 13:240-7.

Mackenbach, Johan P. and Karien Stronks. 2002. "A strategy for tackling health inequalities in the Netherlands." *British Journal of Medicine* 325:1029-32.

National Center for Health Statistics. 2003. Health United States 2003 with Chartbook on the Trends in the Health of Americans. Hyattsville, MD: National Center for Health Statistics.

Nickens, Herbert W. and Jordan J. Cohen. 1996. "On Affirmative Action [Policy Perspectives]." *The Journal of the American Medical Association* 275:572-4.

Oliver, M. L. and T. M. Shapiro. 1997. *Black wealth/White wealth: A new perspective on racial inequality.* New York: Routledge.

Pamuk, E., D. Makuk, K. Heck, and C. Reuben. 1998. *Health, United States, 1998 with Socioeconomic Status and Health Chartbook.* Hyattsville, MD: National Center for Health Statistics.

Politzer, Robert, Jean Yoon, Leiyu Shi, Rhonda Hughes, Jerrilyn Regan, and Marilyn Gaston. 2001. "Inequality in America: The contribution of health centers in reducing and eliminating disparities in access to care." *Medical Care Research and Review* 58:234-48.

Sampson, Robert J. and William J. Wilson. Toward a theory of race, crime, and urban inequality. Ed. Hagan, John and Ruth D. Peterson. *Crime and Inequality.* 37-54. 1995. Stanford, CA, Stanford University Press.

Smedley, Brian D., Adrienne Y. Stith, and Alan R. Nelson. 2003. *Unequal Treatment: Confronting Racial and Ethnic Disparities in Health Care.* Ed. Institute of Medicine. Washington, DC: National Academies Press.

Tekian, Ara. 1997. "A Thematic Review of the Literature on Underrepresented Minorities and Medical Training, 1981-1995: Securing the Foundations of the Bridge to Diversity." *Academic Medicine* 72:S140-S146.

Tucker, Clyde, Ruth McKay, Brian Kojetin, Roderick Harrison, Manuel de la Puente, Linda Stinson, and Ed Robison. 1996. "Testing methods of collecting racial and ethnic information: results of the current population survey supplement on race and ethnicity." *Bureau of Labor Statistical Notes* 40:1-149.

U.S. Department of Health, Education and Welfare. 1979. *Healthy People: The Surgeon General's Report on Health Promotion and Disease Prevention.* DHEW Pub. No. (PHS) 79-55071. Washington, D.C.: United States Government Printing Office.

Williams, David R. 2001. Racial variations in adult health status: Patterns, paradoxes and prospects. In *America Becoming: Racial Trends and Their Consequences.* Eds. Smelser, Neil, William Julius Wilson, and Faith Mitchell. Washington, D.C.: National Academy of Sciences Press.

Williams, David R. and Chiquita Collins. 2003. "Reparations: A viable strategy to address the enigma of African American Health." *American Behavioral Scientist* 46:in press.

Williams, David R. and Chiquita Collins. 1995. "U.S. socioeconomic and racial differences in health." *Annual Review of Sociology* 21:349-86.

Williams, David R., Harold W. Neighbors, and James S. Jackson. 2003. "Racial/ethnic discrimination and health: findings from community studies." *American Journal of Public Health* 93:200-8.

p-Ed

Security Must Never Trump Liberty

By Dennis W. Archer

For more than two years, our nation has lived under the shadow of terrorism, not knowing if or when the next attack will occur. It has been a tense time, with uncertainties and anxiety affecting most aspects of our lives, causing us to focus more than ever before on securing our borders and preparing our police, fire and other emergency response forces.

Without question, these are uncertain times. Our collective sense of security and safety has been shaken. The terrible attacks of September 11, 2001, changed a great deal about this country. They changed the way in which we see ourselves and our place in the world's community of nations, and how we look at one another, within our own borders.

Above all else, they forced us, as Americans, to face who we are as a nation and what we stand for—to weigh the importance of our values and to make changes necessary to protect those values, while also protecting ourselves, our nation and our way of life. One part of that evolution has been the struggle between preserving civil liberties and democratic values and protecting ourselves from terrorists living in foreign lands or on our own soil. In working to achieve an appropriate balance, we have a duty to ensure that the scales never tip too far toward security at the expense of liberty.

Almost immediately after the terrorist attacks of 2001, Americans began to debate whether racial profiling was acceptable. It was a subtle shift away from what until then had been the norm: tacit acceptance and then rebuke of the practice of police and other law enforcement agents to detain individuals on the basis of color. In those first weeks and months after September 11, some proposed that race and ethnicity be used as a way to identify Muslims, Muslim Americans and all who worship Islam as those who would do us harm, demanded curbs on civil liberties and excused even the most vitriolic of racist ideas. But other Americans responded by embracing their neighbors and fellow Americans, helping to protect Islamic places of worship, education and business, and searching to learn more about these communities.

African Americans are all too familiar with the dangers and cost of racial profiling. Many of us have first-hand knowledge of the corrosion of our rights and ways of life that occurs when society makes assumptions about people's character or criminal intent based solely on the color of their skin, the shape of their face or the drape of their clothing. And nearly all of us know that it is not only those individuals and communities targeted by profiling practices, but American society as a whole that pays the price when we allow fear and suspicion to serve as rationalizations for diminishing our foundation of justice and liberty.

The American Bar Association has sought to keep a watchful eye on the effort to define the new balance. It is why, for example, we were so concerned earlier this year when the Inspector General of the Department of Justice issued a report detailing the treatment of immigrants swept up in post September 11 investigations. According to that report, many of these detainees were kept in lockdown 23 hours a day in cells lit at all times. They were denied access to counsel and their families. In fact, the government refused even to identify those in custody and fought court orders requiring them to do so. After being denied bond, most of the detainees were not released for months, even after it became clear that they had no connection to terrorism, because the Justice Department refused to release or deport them until they were cleared by the FBI. The clearance process, which should have taken a few days, took an average of 80 and as many as 244 days to complete.

As troubling as these facts are, they are but one piece of a larger pattern. In fact, one could argue that the systematic violation of these people's basic rights has been one of the most troubling casualties of the war on terrorism. The right to a full, fair and open hearing, the right to have charges filed in a timely manner, the right to legal representation and to confidential conversations with counsel—these are but a few of the basic civil liberties that were denied to immigrants in the wake of September 11.

It is this concern, as well, that informs the ABA's misgivings about the possible use of military tribunals to try terrorists. The question of whether and how military tribunals could be used is one that has stirred much debate in the legal community. The initial Military Order establishing the tribunals was very broad, and many lawyers thought it threatened the fundamental concepts of justice and due process.

So when the Department of Defense issued procedural rules for civilian defense counsel in military tribunals earlier this year, and announced that trials for six of the detainees being held at Guantanamo Bay could begin shortly, the ABA undertook a careful review. Unfortunately, we found that the rules were crafted in a way that would unfairly undermine the ability of civilian defense counsel who represent detainees to render zealous, competent and effective assistance to their clients. As a result, the Association is on record arguing that the government:

- should not monitor privileged conversations, or interfere with confidential communications, between defense counsel and clients;
- should allow defense counsel to be present at all stages of tribunal proceedings and should have access to all information necessary to prepare a defense;
- should ensure that defense counsel be able to consult with other lawyers and seek expert assistance, advice or counsel outside the defense team; and
- should not limit the ability of defense counsel to speak publicly, consistent with the Model Rules of Professional Conduct and their duty not to reveal classified or protected information.

To date, there have been no military tribunals. But should they occur, it is critical that every appropriate effort be made to ensuring that these detainees are afforded effective representation. The world will be watching to see how the United States, long the exemplar of liberty and due process, treats these detainees.

Also unsettling is the fact that the challenges to our rights and liberties have not been limited to immigrants and foreign detainees, as witnessed by the treatment of two U.S. citizens picked up and held in the United States as enemy combatants in connection with terrorist plots. If these two are guilty, every effort must be made to ensure that they are brought to justice and punished. But it must be done in the American way. These U.S. citizens must have access to counsel and to the courts.

This is not to suggest that American citizens should never be held as enemy combatants. But there must be guidelines for such detention, guidelines that ensure that they enjoy the protection of the U.S. Constitution, and that they have access to counsel and to meaningful judicial review of their status. Failure to do so would be to tear at the Bill of Rights, the very fabric of our great democracy, and erode our cherished constitutional safeguards.

What is critical now—and must be done on an ongoing basis—is vigorous review of the new policies and procedures that we adopt in fighting the war on terror. The administration and Congress must work together to ensure that our civil liberties are not the greatest casualty in the war.

Most important, we must be ever vigilant that our actions and our policies attest to who we are and what we stand for. We must not abandon our Constitution, our Bill of Rights or our fundamental beliefs. Rather, our democratic principles should guide us as we make decisions about how to proceed in these challenging times. We owe it to ourselves, to our history and to the generations that succeed us to work together to ensure that our society remains free and fair, and that our democratic values prevail.

The Empowerment Movement and the Black Male

By JAMES R. LANIER

The public image of and discourse about African-American males in American society is characterized by strikingly contrasting colors of success and failure.

In the news and editorial columns of the mainstream media; on the airwaves of the broadcast media, and in academia as well, we are bombarded, on the one hand, with images of larger-than-life African-American males excelling in nearly every area of American life—but especially so in the fields of athletics and entertainment.

However, we are also simultaneously bombarded to a much greater extent with stark images of black males *in extremis*—in poverty, poor health, apathy, and being disproportionately arrested and incarcerated. Reducing the yawning gaps between the sector of African-American males who are doing well and those who are not is a formidable challenge for both Black America and the larger American society as a whole. Their failure to overcome this challenge—and it is a task both must tackle—will produce disastrous consequences for both.

In fact, the paradox in status and image that envelops the image of the African-American male reflects the status of Black Americans as a group.

As a group and as individuals, blacks have made enormous advances since the victories of the Civil Rights Years of the 1950s and 1960s: in their matriculation in higher education and expansion of the black middle class; and in their advancement to the highest levels of responsibility in academia, the corporate world, medicine and the law, the nonprofit sector, the arts, and government. The names of the individuals whose accomplishments have led or symbolized the breakthroughs in these fields are, by and large, well known.

And yet, other facts and statistics underscore how far America remains from eliminating the substantial differences of what is glibly referred to as America's racial divide.

For example, two years ago in the pages of this publication, Franklin D. Raines, chairman and CEO of Fannie Mae, and a National Urban League trustee, presented statistics about a number of areas to show what American society would look like "if the average black American enjoyed the same status as the average white American."

Among other things, Raines determined that if parity existed between blacks and whites, the average black American household would see its annual income rise by 56 percent, the wealth of black households would rise by 1 trillion dollars, two million more African Americans would have their high school diplomas and two million more their undergraduate degrees. Raines also declared that if a black-white parity existed, there'd be 700,000 fewer African American adults and 33,000 fewer juveniles incarcerated—at a savings to the country of more than $15 billion.

Marc H. Morial, the new president and CEO of the National Urban League, referred to these and other facts and statistics in his main address to the League's annual conference last summer. "America is a paradox of progress," Morial said. "While the Civil Rights Movement defeated Jim Crow ... there's still an equality gap in this nation."

"If the 19th century was about a Freedom Movement to end that peculiar institution known as slavery," he went on, "and the 20th century was about a Civil Rights Movement to defeat Jim Crow and achieve equal rights and social justice for those who a century ago had been freed from the bondage of slavery, then I say [the Urban League] ... must lead a new movement—an Empowerment Movement—to close the Equality Gap."

Morial said the League intends to back up its words with a concerted program of action developed in part by its commission on the status of African-American males. The commission, comprised of a diverse group of scholars, practitioners, and community leaders, will convene later this year to begin a two-year study of African-American male life; its purpose is to develop recommendations to improve the status of African-American males at every level of society, and thereby improve the quality of life for Black America and America as a whole. Morial said he expects the 100-plus Urban League affiliates around the country to play a crucial role in implementing the commission's recommendations and using the effort to spark broader related efforts in their local communities.

Of course, the Urban League has hardly been the only organization to recognize the need for action in this area. Two other efforts are the D.C. Commission on Black Men and Boys, organized in 2001 principally by Congresswoman Eleanor Holmes Norton, Democrat of the District of Columbia, and the State of the African-American Male Conference, organized last year principally by Representative Danny Davis, Democrat of Illinois. The former is concerned exclusively with Washington, D.C.; the latter is national in scope.

To be blunt, the problems affecting African-American males span the spectrum; but I'll focus on three.

The U.S. Department of Education's report, *Education of Blacks*, is one of many that depict the alarming difficulties black children and youth endure in far too many schools. The overwhelming majority of black elementary and secondary pupils attend predominantly minority schools which are located in troubled neighborhoods, have inadequate resources, and are too often staffed with inexperienced teachers. A greater percentage of black pupils—15 percent of all black school students—are enrolled in special education classes, compared to the 11 percent of their white counterparts; and blacks' rate of suspension, 35 percent, far exceeds the 15 percent for whites. The federal document concludes, not surprisingly, that black students fail a grade and drop out more often than whites, and score lower on standardized tests. Although, distressingly, the number of black girls falling into this pit is increasing, black boys and young males endure it most often.

One reason such statistics are alarming is that, far more than whites, dropping out of school puts black males on a treadmill to danger: Princeton University researchers Bruce Western and Becky Petit, looking at data for 1999, found that 52.1 percent of black men aged 30 to 34, who had dropped out of high school had prison records compared to 13 percent of white men of the same age group who had failed to complete high school. It's likely that the so-called school reform movement, with its rigid emphasis on standardized testing will exacerbate the difficulties black students, and particularly black males endure in the nation's schools.

In the workplace, albeit the high visibility of a small group of African-American male achievers in business, black males as a group lag significantly behind their white counterparts at all levels. Black males (and females, too, of course) still encounter significant discrimination in hiring and promotion, and in gaining the same level of pay as their white counterparts when they have equal levels of education and work experience. As a result, the median earned income for black men is $25,551, compared to $32,151 for their white counterparts.

The starkest illustration of the very different fortunes in mass terms of black and white males in the economy is seen in their unemployment rates. As this volume goes to press, the latest monthly unemployment-rate comparisons, for January 2004, illustrate the historical relationship: the black-male unemployment rate of 10.5 percent was more than twice the 4.9-percent rate of white males. In addition, a recent report of the National Urban League Institute for Opportunity and Equality determined that black males who lose their jobs are likely to remain unemployed longer than white males—a particularly serious dynamic today given that the "jobless recovery" has pushed the numbers of those unemployed for longer than 26 weeks to all-time records.

Furthermore, the severity of the black-male employment situation becomes even more worrisome when one considers the extraordinary number (818,900 compared to 630,700 white men) of black males incarcerated in jails and state and federal prisons.

This increasing imprisoning of African-American males—even as crime rates continue to decline—is one of the most astonishing dynamics in the world today. Although black males are only about six percent of the total U.S. population, they comprise slightly more than 44 percent of America's prison and jail inmates. By contrast, white males, and Hispanic-American males, who are nearly 37 percent and about 7 percent of the American population, respectively, comprise 34 percent and nearly 19 percent, respectively, of prison and jail inmates. These black prisoners (the number of black females being incarcerated has risen sharply in recent years, too) represent a tremendous, continuing loss of economic, social and political "human capital" for Black America—and the problem may get even worse. Experts predict that if incarceration rates remain the same, 1 in 3 black males born in 2001 will be incarcerated at some time in their lives (compared to less than 6 percent of whites males born that year). One can expect the instability already tragically apparent in numerous impoverished black neighborhoods to radiate outward with ever more serious results—unless steps are taken to prevent the looming disaster. In fact, what needs to be done is largely known, and can be succinctly stated.

The public schools and black civic society—black parents, and the network of black organizations at the local and national levels—have to motivate and teach black males to achieve academically. Skill-based job training must be made available for those uninterested in immediately pursuing academically focused higher learning. There should be swift and harsh punishment for employers who are found to discriminate against anyone. The criminal justice system needs wholesale reform, including repeal of mandatory sentencing regulations and a return to judges of discretion in sentencing; alternatives to incarceration for most low-level drug offenders; and an equalization of the penalties for possession and distribution of crack and powder cocaine.

All of these sketched suggestions, and many more, are planks of the "Empowerment Movement" Marc H. Morial outlined at last summer's National Urban League Conference. His point then was not so much to delineate details as to have his listeners adopt an attitude, a joint commitment to pursue aiding both those who have benefited from th civil rights victories of the past four decades and those who have yet to benefit at all.

The vision of such a joint commitment is rooted in the reality that what poor black males and the black poor in general need most aren't tendentious lectures about the value of work. What they need most *is the opportunity to work.*

That truth was dramatically illustrated in 1999 and 2000 when, at what in hindsight was the end of the 1990s economic boom, the black unemployment fell to a record low of 7 percent. It fell for two reasons.

One was that the demand for workers at the low-wage service sector of the high-flying economy was so great that those jobs, finally, opened up for low-skilled, poorly-educated black males. The second was that those males—the primary targets for more than three decades of the culture-of-poverty thesis—rushed to fill them. Writing of the landmark event, *Washington Post* columnist E. J. Dionne remarked, "those who argued for years that the plight of the poor owed more to what was wrong with the economy than to what was wrong with the poor have been proved right." And Princeton professor Jennifer L. Hochschild told a *New York Times* reporter: "Poor blacks never lost faith in work, education and individual effort. What's different now is that they can do something about it."

That's the major truth those in the Empowerment Movement have to keep in mind as they set their sights on expanding opportunity to poor black males—America's great untapped resource.

The Transformation of the Welfare Caseload

By Kenya L. Covington

Seldom are the more than four million children who receive cash assistance as a child-only case or as part of a family the primary focus of welfare policy discussions. Rarely does such a discussion even occur—except when tough policy stances are being proposed to decrease teenage pregnancy, increase the involvement of their fathers in their rearing, or leverage greater funding for child care as compromises toward passage of a welfare bill. Otherwise, the growing proportion of children in the Temporary Assistance to Needy Families (TANF) program and the resulting need to expand the focus of services funded by it are largely ignored

It should not be. A well-intentioned welfare policy must acknowledge the drastic changes in the composition of the public assistance caseload. The overall composition of families with dependent children on the TANF (once known as Aid to Families with Dependent Children) rolls has changed drastically since 1990: TANF is increasingly serving more children as a proportion of all recipients. In 2001, children on the rolls, who receive cash benefits as part of the family comprised about 75 percent of the entire caseload. However, child-only cases accounted for a full 35 percent of the entire caseload; in just four years, there was an 8-percent increase in the proportion of all children on the caseload. Moreover, many people are unaware that the composition of child-only cases—meaning there is no adult recipient included in the TANF cash grant—continued to grow even more acutely following the TANF program's full implementation.

There are various reasons that children become child-only cases. About 23 percent of children in child-only cases are in the custody of non-parental caregivers, primarily through the foster care system. Another 14 percent are child-only cases because the parent is not an American citizen: the 1996 welfare reform legislation included stringent provisions against adult non-citizens receiving assistance. Another 14 percent are child-only because the parent is receiving Supplemental Social Insurance, and in about 4 percent of cases the parent was barred from assistance, or "sanctioned off," for not complying with regulations.

Although the total child welfare caseload has declined by more than 4.3 million since 1996, a 50-percent drop, the decline for white children outpaced that for African-American and Latino-American children by 12 percent and 26 percent, respectively. Now, the number of African-American children, 1.7 million, dominate the child welfare rolls and the 1.2 million Latino children on the rolls indicates they are a growing proportion as well.

Unfortunately, several current proposals before Congress ignore the new trends that indicate welfare has become a child-recipient dominated program. One proposal calls for single mothers with children under 6 years of age to work 40 hours. Another would require that states impose a full-family sanction for work noncompliance. At present, about sixteen states and the District of Columbia provide the child with cash benefits even if their adult guardian has been barred for non-compliance. Yet, some proposals now under consideration would require states to impose a full-family sanction—revoking the entire value of the cash benefit—against families not meeting state requirements.

It is more humane for states to choose what policy option to utilize rather than legislating a universal policy option. Full sanctions are very harsh and in every situation children would bear the brunt of the penalty. Undoubtedly, absent no sanction, a partial sanction is best when considering the well-being of children. Despite the continued cash benefit the child receives, there are various concerns even with the partial sanction. Even though the household will continue to receive a portion of the cash benefit, the most likely scenario is that the adult recipient will have fewer resources to work with—resulting in less food, no child care, or substandard housing.

One benefit of lingering welfare dependence for children is their access to health insurance. Under current law, all children receiving cash benefits are also eligible to receive Medicaid. Typically, family poverty translates into poor access to health insurance. However, recent reports from the U.S. Census suggest that despite overall increases in the number of low-income people uninsured, the uninsured child population has decreased. Both access to health insurance by child recipients and the State Children's Health Insurance Program (S-CHIP) are important resources and likely contributed substantially to increasing the number of children who are insured.

Racial disparities in the decline of the child caseload further underscore the need to shape welfare policy so that it helps children and adolescents who are on welfare either because their adult guardians haven't yet been able to become self-sufficient, or because of other circumstances.

In other words, simplistically using the decline of the number of Americans on welfare as the measure of TANF's success—especially now that the program primarily consists of children—is not valid. The overall quality of life, including the health, education and living arrangements for the children of adult recipients and child-only cases must all be taken into account. Despite the necessary difference in the way children and adult recipients are treated, it remains imperative that the government provide comprehensive services to the entire household.

Furthermore, because African Americans and Latino Americans make up a growing proportion of welfare recipients, it's critical that race and ethnicity be part of the measuring process. The evidence is strong that racial discrimination has contributed to notable racial disparities in the ability of welfare recipients to get jobs, and thus, in who has remained on the welfare rolls.

Such scholars as Susan Gooden, of Virginia Tech, and Ronald Walters, of the University of Maryland, have documented the differences in how caseworkers treat African-American and white female adult recipients.

Others have found a strong correlation between harsh welfare policies and the percentage of blacks on the rolls. Obviously because any discriminatory treatment also affects the children within these households, one may rightly fear that as the rolls become much blacker and browner, welfare regulations will become more punitive even towards children.

Finally, although the incidence of child poverty has declined since the early 1990s for children of every racial and ethnic group, not all families benefited. In fact, the number of families facing extreme poverty increased and more children lived in single-parent, extremely poor families in 1998 than in 1996. Most recently with the economic bust occurring in the early 2000s, the percent of children in poverty began to creep up most strikingly for African-American children. Thus, it's even more crucial to invest in "at risk" youth in ways that aid their cognitive development, overall healthiness, and prospects for a stable home environment that simply reducing the adult welfare caseload will never do.

p-Ed

Five Things You Must Have to Run a Successful Business

By Melinda F. Emerson

Young people are always told that they should go to college to get a good job. This statement is generally true, but the world is bigger than a good job. To borrow a phrase from my mentor, Bill Mays of Mays Chemical, "The only way to build true wealth in America is through entrepreneurship."

Now that doesn't mean that you shouldn't ever work for someone, but it does mean that when you take a job, you should learn all you can—meaning everyone else's job too—and have an exit strategy. If you're set on being an entrepreneur, the only reason to deviate from this plan is if you're on the management success track in Corporate America (and even in that case, entrepreneurship could be considered a Plan B for almost anyone.

There are five things you must have to start and run a successful business:

- A solid business idea
- A current business plan
- Good credit
- A good understanding of customer service
- A supportive family/spouse (especially on those hard days when there's no money and plenty of work to do); and,
- A passion for what you do. (It'll be the only thing that keeps you going.)

Do have a solid business idea

Solid business ideas can appear from anywhere: Sometimes, people turn their hobbies into businesses; others buy existing businesses, or buy into franchises; and some are pushed to create their business ideas out of a desperate necessity. Ideally, your business venture should be something you have a degree in or have been trained in professionally. As a rule of thumb, I suggest working for a business like the one you want to start for a few years, before jumping out there on your own. For example, don't start a daycare center if you've never worked with kids just because you think you can make a lot of money. Also, remember that it generally takes four to five years to get a business up and running on its own—and that what makes the difference between you and your competition is how well you run your company. My favorite example of this is Wal-Mart: They don't sell the best jeans or sneakers on the market, but they are the number one retailer in the world because the company is run with military precision. They have a zero tolerance policy on late shipments from suppliers. One mistake will cause a supplier to be eliminated in all Wal-Mart stores worldwide. Most suppliers can't afford not to be in Wal-Mart stores. They are a $250 billion operation because of their ability to run their business.

Do have a business plan

It takes a special kind of person to be a successful entrepreneur. (Notice that I did not say just "entrepreneur.") Success is a formula in business. Everyone has great ideas, but ideas do not become businesses until they are completely thought out and written down in the form of a business plan. I meet people all the time who tell me they are thinking about starting a business. My first reaction is "Great! Have you started writing your business plan yet?" A business plan is essential for a successful business. Think of it like this: You'd never take a trip without knowing such things as your itinerary, mode of transportation, travel time, length of stay, and cost. So why would you start a business without knowing the same kind of information? For help in understanding how to write a business plan, check with the federal Small Business

Administration, which runs seminars and workshops, or you might also check with your local small business development center, or purchase business plan software from an office supply store. Once you've begun to implement your business plan, review it every six months or so to determine whether to revise it based on your actual business experience.

Do have good credit

As an entrepreneur, when you first start out in business, your personal credit is your business credit. So if you have credit problems, it'll be almost impossible to gain access to start-up capital. Also, remember that if you intend to borrow in order to buy into a franchise, you must have collateral and at least 10 to 20 percent of the needed operating capital before a bank will give you a loan. Banks want to see that you've committed a good chunk of your resources to the enterprise, too. Angel investors and venture capital funds are an option; but only high growth companies that will be traded on the stock exchange or sold to a large competitor really appeal to this audience: They want to recoup their initial investment with significant interest within five years. Furthermore, if they invest, they'll own a sizable stake in the company—which often means they'll take an active role in management in order to protect their investment. The majority of minority companies do not appeal to this audience.

Customer service is key

There are times in business when you will mess up. It happens to everyone, the key is how do you fix it. Once a client called me the day after Christmas in a fury because they hadn't received their videotapes. "We've paid you all your money," she complained, "so where is our merchandise!!" I was stunned because I had directed a subcontractor to my firm to duplicate the copies and deliver them before Thanksgiving; and they had assured me they had. I quickly apologized and told my client I'd make sure they had their tapes by the end of that week. I then tracked down my subcontractor, told him bluntly that no excuses would do, picked up my videotapes and personally delivered them to my client—

along with a fruit basket to underscore how much I valued our relationship. To this day, that client is still a client—and I never called that subcontractor again.

The point is that customer service is critical to the success of a small business and you must be absolutely sure that everyone representing you treats your customers as well as you do. If you can't be sure they will, run as fast as you can in the opposite direction.

Have a supportive spouse and family

When you're first starting a business, it's a good idea to plan on significantly scaling back personal expenses. Consider things like lavish vacations, new cars or new clothes unrealistic for the short term. Make sure you tell your spouse and family about your goals and ambitions because you'll need their understanding and support. This is critical, because your spouse may need to become the sole breadwinner for a while. You'll also need them to have a positive outlook, and cheer you up on days when things don't go well; so, always keep the overall goal in front of everyone. This is particularly true if you need your family to help out by working in the business. Sustaining a small business is a tough, long road. Without positive people around you, it will be that much harder.

Business ownership is a viable, necessary option for African Americans. It's not easy, and not everyone can be, or should be an entrepreneur. But more African Americans need to consider the challenge. If you have a plan, seek training, ask for help, be nice to people, and pray along the way, then you have a good chance of succeeding. More than likely, success won't come overnight but having a positive family environment will give you the staying power to run the marathon of starting and running a small business.

Gaps, Traps and Lies: African-American Students and Test Scores

By Ronald O. Ross

High-quality schooling involves so much more than just the calculation of test scores in reading and mathematics. Public schools are supposed to build children's academic, social vocational and personal skills, too—and the humanities, arts, music and the study of foreign languages can make an important contribution to that.

But you'd never know it from the way such buzzwords of the current craze for high-stakes testing as "assessment," "average yearly progress,"and "accountability" now rule the discussion about public education.

Since 1983 when "A Nation At Risk," the authoritative federal report on America's public schools sounded the alarm about "…a rising tide of mediocrity that threatens our very future as a Nation and a people," and called for a renewed commitment to the twin goals of equity and high-quality schooling, critics from the left, right and center have demanded that the schools meet the challenge.

The problem is, however, that the current, obsessive focus on testing is likely to have some profoundly negative consequences.

One area where that has already become clear is the seemingly endlessly discussed black-white achievement gap on standardized tests.

As usual when it comes to racial issues, blacks' performance on these tests receives the full, questioning glare of the spotlight, while that of whites, and other groups, too, to a significant extent, is made nearly invisible.

That is, while black students' performance on these tests is dissected in the mainstream media and at educational conferences in terms of class, regional and even country-of-origin backgrounds, the performance of white and other students is not. Indeed, a kind of linguistic sleight-of-hand is invoked when discussing non-black test takers. It's strongly implied, particularly for whites and Asian-Americans, that there is no test-score differentiation among their various sub-groups, and that all of their test-takers do well on standardized tests—even though the test scores themselves irrefutably show that's not so.

Plumbing the 2002 scores of the Scholastic Aptitude Test, perhaps the best known of all standardized tests, offers a cogent example of what's often left out of the discussions about the black-white test-score gap at every level.

According to an important article in the Autumn 2002 issue of the *Journal of Blacks in Higher Education*, the average combined score for African-American students who took the 2002 SAT was 857—203 points lower than the 1,060 average combined score for whites.

Even more startling at first glance is the gap between those whites and blacks who score above 700 on the mathematics and verbal sections of the test—the test-score threshold level for the nation's highly-ranked colleges and universities.

Of the 122,684 black students who took the 2002 SATs, only 838 scored 700 or better on the math and only 822 scored 700 or better on the verbal sections of the test, respectively.

Those numbers are dwarfed by the number of white students who performed that well: 43,002 white students scored 700 or better on the test's mathematics section, and 35,723 whites did so on the verbal.

(The gaps are similar for the ACT, or American College Testing program examinations, which are also used for college admissions. About 120,000 black students took the ACTs in 2002.)

These are sobering statistics; and they, and others which emphasize the lagging performance of blacks on standardized tests, are continually cited as evidence of a lack of aspiration for education within Black America.

But, as usual when examining the racial gaps between black and white Americans, there's a lot more here that's important than meets the eye.

For example, one SAT reality that's almost never discussed is the surprisingly small percentage of white students who score at or above 700.

To be sure, their absolute numbers are large. But the 35,723 white students who score 700 or better on the verbal section make up just 5.1 percent of the more than 714,000 white students who took the 2002 SATs. The 43,002 high scorers on the mathematics section were just 6.2 percent of white test takers.

If white students as a group have so many more advantages than black students—as they do—why don't more of them score higher on the SATs? What are the characteristics of the white students who don't do well on the Does it break down along regional lines? Or class lines? Or income lines? Or quality of schooling? Or ethnicity? Or some combination of all of the above?

Another question: Why is the discussion about poor pupil performance on the SATs focused entirely on African Americans? If we are to be concerned that more than 98 percent of African Americans score below 700 on the tests, should we not also be concerned that more than 94 percent of white students do, too?

Much of the discourse about the black-white achievement gap ignores the fact that from 1976 to 1988 the gap in SAT scores between blacks and whites closed significantly. In fact, the progress blacks made was so compelling that it was widely expected the gap would soon disappear altogether. Instead, it began to widen again.

Why?

Was one factor the widening inequality between blacks and whites in income and wealth that occurred during the 1980s? We know, as the JBHE article states, there's a "direct correlation between family income and SAT scores. For both blacks and whites, as income goes up, so do test scores."

Yet, while 24 percent of the white students who took the 2002 SATs came from families with annual incomes of $100,000 or higher, just 5 percent of black test-takers did. Conversely, while just 5 percent of white test-takers came from families with annual incomes below $20,000, 28 percent of black test-takers did.

Much of the public discourse about the black-white test gap also ignores the fact that black children in predominantly black schools—which the overwhelming number of African-American children attend—are in profound ways locked in a struggle for their very physical and psychological survival.

Their schools—overwhelmingly in poor neighborhoods—are likely to be poorly maintained and also characterized by a dumbed-down curriculum, outdated textbooks, high teacher turnover, and a large number of teachers with less than five years teaching experience. Their neighborhoods are likely to endure high rates of unemployment and crime, a poor tax base and physical infrastructure, inferior access to public services, and too few two-parent homes.

Few white youth have to navigate the kind of school and neighborhood environments a majority of black youngsters—whether they come from stable or unstable homes—face.

For many of the latter, it's graphically clear that survival, not education, is the top priority. That that knowledge and its harsh reality can exact a great toll on students' readiness and ability to pay attention to their schoolwork should be obvious.

As the JBHE article makes clear, these factors describe the enormous educational disadvantage most black students—even those from middle-income families—endure five decades after the concerted effort of the civil rights movement to gain quality, integrated schooling for black children seemed to find a solution in the *Brown* decision.

One of the ways in which that disadvantage comes home to roost directly is in the test score gap between black and white students.

Many of the remedies to this systemic neglect of the scholastic development of black schoolchildren are obvious.

For one thing, our colleges and universities must provide the scholarship funds and other incentives to lure more top-quality undergraduates into teaching. Once hired, teachers ought to be supported with the kind of sponsored professional development programs that give them opportunities to polish old skills and develop new ones. And we should pay teachers more for their expertise—in part so we can demand that all teachers meet the exacting standards we should impose, for the sake of the children, on every teacher.

Of course, these and other reforms that have as their goal producing more skilled teachers for America's black and Latino children are expensive. But they are far less expensive, in both monetary and human terms, than the cost of continued neglect.

Testing of student's' abilities is not going to go away, nor, used properly, should it. Yet, there is precious little evidence from those who most loudly tout the need for the schools' high-stakes testing that they're willing to put the necessary dollars up to transform public education.

Not until that happens will we have driven a stake through the heart of the achievement gap that separates so many black children from educational opportunity.

And, in fact, we can draw from the statistics of the Scholastic Aptitude Test itself an extraordinarily powerful wellspring of inspiration for this task.

For those statistics show that, despite their low family incomes, inadequate school facilities, inferior curricula, and, too often, teachers and guidance counselors who have no faith in them—black high school students have continued to take these tests in their zealous pursuit of higher education.

If these youngsters can battle against the enormous odds they face, can we do less?

History of the
National Urban League

The National Urban League, which has played so pivotal a role in the 20th-Century Freedom Movement, grew out of that spontaneous grassroots movement for freedom and opportunity that came to be called the Black Migrations. When the U.S. Supreme Court declared its approval of segregation in the 1896 *Plessy v. Ferguson* decision, the brutal system of economic, social and political oppression the White South quickly adopted rapidly transformed what had been a trickle of African Americans northward into a flood.

Those newcomers to the North soon discovered that while they had escaped the South, they had not escaped racial discrimination. Excluded from all but menial jobs in the larger society, victimized by poor housing and education, and inexperienced in the ways of urban living, many lived in terrible social and economic conditions.

Still, in the degree of difference between South and North lay opportunity, and that African Americans clearly understood.

But to capitalize on that opportunity, to successfully adapt to urban life and to reduce the pervasive discrimination they faced, they would need help. That was the reason the Committee on Urban Conditions Among Negroes was established on September 29, 1910 in New York City. Central to the organization's founding were two remarkable people: Mrs. Ruth Standish Baldwin and Dr. George Edmund Haynes, who would become the Committee's first executive secretary. Mrs. Baldwin, the widow of a railroad magnate and a member of one of America's oldest families, had a remarkable social conscience and was a stalwart champion of the poor and disadvantaged. Dr. Haynes, a graduate of Fisk University, Yale University, and Columbia University (he was the first African American to receive a doctorate from that institution), felt a compelling need to use his training as a social worker to serve his people.

A year later, the Committee merged with the Committee for the Improvement of Industrial Conditions Among Negroes in New York (founded in New York in 1906), and the National League for the Protection of Colored Women (founded in 1905) to form the National League on Urban Conditions Among Negroes. In 1920, the name was later shortened to the National Urban League.

The interracial character of the League's board was set from its first days. Professor Edwin R. A. Seligman of Columbia University, one of the leaders in progressive social service activities in New York City, served as chairman from 1911 to 1913. Mrs. Baldwin took the post until 1915.

The fledgling organization counseled black migrants from the South, helped train black social workers, and worked in various other ways to bring educational and employment opportunities to blacks. Its research into the problems blacks faced in employment opportunities, recreation, housing, health and sanitation, and education spurred the League's quick growth. By the end of World War I the organization had 81 staff members working in 30 cities.

In 1918, Dr. Haynes was succeeded by Eugene Kinckle Jones who would direct the agency until his retirement in 1941. Under his direction, the League significantly expanded its multifaceted campaign to crack the barriers to black employment, spurred first by the boom years of the 1920s, and then, by the desperate years of the Great Depression. Efforts at reasoned persuasion were buttressed by boycotts against firms that refused to employ blacks, pressures on schools to expand vocational opportunities for young people, constant prodding of Washington officials to include blacks in New Deal recovery programs and a drive to get blacks into previously segregated labor unions.

As World War II loomed, Lester Granger, a seasoned League veteran and crusading newspaper columnist, was appointed Jones' successor. Outspoken in his commitment to advancing opportunity for African Americans, Granger pushed tirelessly to integrate the racist trade unions, and led the League's effort to support A. Philip Randolph's March on Washington Movement to fight discrimination in defense work and in the armed services. Under Granger, the League, through its own Industrial Relations Laboratory, had notable success in cracking the color bar in numerous defense plants. The nation's demand for civilian labor during the war also helped the organization press ahead with greater urgency its programs to train black youths for meaningful blue-collar employment. After the war those efforts expanded to persuading Fortune 500 companies to hold career conferences on the campuses of Negro Colleges and place blacks in upper-echelon jobs.

Of equal importance to the League's own future sources of support, Granger avidly supported the organization of its volunteer auxiliary, the National Urban League Guild, which, under the leadership of Mollie Moon, became an important national force in its own right.

The explosion of the civil rights movement provoked a change for the League, one personified by its new leader, Whitney M. Young, Jr., who became executive director in 1961. A social worker like his predecessors, he substantially expanded the League's fund-raising ability—and, most critically, made the League a full partner in the civil rights movement. Indeed, although the League's tax-exempt status barred it from protest activities, it hosted at its New York headquarters the planning meetings of A. Philip Randolph, Martin Luther King, Jr., and other civil rights leaders for the 1963 March on Washington. Young was also a forceful advocate for greater government and private-sector efforts to eradicate poverty. His call for a domestic Marshall Plan, a ten-point program designed to close the gap between the huge social and economic gap between black and white Americans, significantly influenced the discussion of the Johnson Administration's War on Poverty legislation.

Young's tragic death in 1971 in a drowning incident off the coast of Lagos, Nigeria brought another change in leadership. Vernon E. Jordan, Jr., formerly Executive Director of the United Negro College Fund, took over as the League's fifth Executive Director in 1972 (the title of the office was changed to President in 1977).

For the next decade, until his resignation in December 1981, Jordan skillfully guided the League to new heights of achievement. He oversaw a major expansion of its social-service efforts, as the League became a significant conduit for the federal government to establish programs and deliver services to aid urban communities, and brokered fresh initiatives in such League programs as housing, health, education and minority business development. Jordan also instituted a citizenship education program that helped increase the black vote and brought new programs to such areas as energy, the environment, and non-traditional jobs for women of color—and he developed *The State of Black America* report.

In 1982, John E. Jacob, a former chief executive officer of the Washington, D.C. and San Diego affiliates who had served as Executive Vice President, took the reins of leadership, solidifying the League's internal structure and expanding its outreach even further.

Jacob established the Permanent Development Fund in order to increase the organization's financial stamina. In honor of Whitney Young, he established several programs to aid the development of those who work for and with the League: The Whitney M. Young, Jr. Training Center, to provide training and leadership development opportunities for both staff and volunteers; the Whitney M. Young, Jr. Race Relations Program, which recognizes affiliates doing exemplary work in race relations; and the Whitney M. Young, Jr. Commemoration Ceremony, which honors and pays tribute to long term staff and volunteers who have made extraordinary contributions to the Urban League Movement. Jacob established the League's NULITES youth-development program and spurred the League to put new emphasis on programs to reduce teenage pregnancy, help single female heads of households, combat crime in black communities, and increase voter registration.

Hugh B. Price, appointed to the League's top office in July 1994, took its reins at a critical moment for the League, for Black America, and for the nation as a whole. The fierce market-driven dynamic known as "globalization," swept the world, fundamentally altering economic relations among and within countries, including the United States. Price, a lawyer by training, with extensive experience in community development and other public policy issues, intensified the organization's work in three broad areas: in education and youth development, in individual and community-wide economic empowerment, and in the forceful advocacy of affirmative action and the promotion of inclusion as a critical foundation for securing America's future as a multi-ethnic democracy.

In the spring of 2003, Price stepped down after a productive nine-year tenure, and Marc H. Morial, the former two-term Mayor of New Orleans, Louisiana, was appointed president and chief executive officer.

With the economic gains Black America had forged during the 1990s threatened by the post-9/11 jobs crisis and the country's "jobless recovery," Morial's mandate has been to aggressively guide the Urban League to the forefront of the new policy actions and the new public discourse that this first decade of the new century demand. He has responded with an energetic program to re-shape the organization to lead an Empowerment Movement to reduce the "equality gaps" that bedevil Black America and the nation in five critical areas: in education, economic matters, health and the quality of life, in issues of civic engagement, and in civil rights and racial justice.

"Forty years ago," Morial said during his Keynote Address at the 2003 National Urban League Conference in Pittsburgh, his first as the organization's head, "a great generation of Americans led a movement that made America's present possible. The task for us, their beneficiaries, is to marshal the courage and conviction, the fortitude and the fight, the intelligence and the integrity they displayed to complete their work."

 *appendix II*

Index of Authors and Articles, 1987-2004

In 1987, the National Urban League began publishing *The State of Black America* in a smaller, typeset format. By so doing, it became easier to catalog and archive the various essays by author and article name.

The 2004 edition of *The State of Black America* is the tenth to contain an index of the authors and articles that have appeared since 1987. The articles have been divided by topic and are listed in the alphabetical order of their authors' names.

Reprints of the articles catalogued herein are available through the National Urban League, 120 Wall Street, New York, New York 10005; 212/558-5316.

Affirmative Action

Special Section. "Affirmative Action/National Urban League Columns and Amici Brief on the Michigan Case," **2003**, pp. 225–268.

Afterword

Daniels, Lee A., "Praising the Mutilated World," **2002**, pp. 181-188

AIDS

Rockeymoore, Maya, "AIDS in Black America and the World," **2002**, pp. 123-146

Black Males

Lanier, James R., "The Empowerment Movement and the Black Male," **2004**, pp. 143-148.

Business

Emerson, Melinda F., "Five Things You Must Have to Run a Successful Business," **2004**, pp. 153–156.

Glasgow, Douglas G., "The Black Underclass in Perspective," **1987**, pp. 129–144.

Henderson, Lenneal J., "Empowerment through Enterprise: African-American Business Development," **1993**, pp. 91–108.

Price, Hugh B., "Beacons in a New Millennium: Reflections on 21st-Century Leaders and Leadership," **2000**, pp. 13–39.

Tidwell, Billy J., "Black Wealth: Facts and Fiction," **1988**, pp. 193–210.

Walker, Juliet E.K., "The Future of Black Business in America: Can It Get Out of the Box?," **2000**, pp. 199-226.

Children and Youths

Cox, Kenya L. Covington, "The Childcare Imbalance: Impact on WorkingOpportunities for Poor Mothers," **2003**, pp.197–224d.

Fulbright-Anderson, Karen,, "Developing Our Youth: What Works," **1996**, pp. 127–143.

Hare, Bruce R., "Black Youth at Risk," **1988**, pp. 81–93.

Howard, Jeff P., "The Third Movement: Developing Black Children for the 21st Century," **1993**, pp. 11–34.

McMurray, Georgia L. "Those of Broader Vision: An African-American Perspective on Teenage Pregnancy and Parenting," **1990**, pp. 195–211.

Moore, Evelyn K., "The Call: Universal Child Care," **1996**, pp. 219–244.

Scott, Kimberly A., "A Case Study: African-American Girls and Their Families," 2003, pp. 181–195.

Williams, Terry M., and William Kornblum, "A Portrait of Youth: Coming of Age in Harlem Public Housing," **1991**, pp. 187–207.

Civil Rights

Archer, Dennis W., "Security Must Never Trump Liberty," **2004**, pp. 139–142.

Ogletree, Jr., Charles J., "Brown at 50: Considering the Continuing Legal Struggle for Racial Justice," **2004**, pp. 81–96.

Criminal Justice

Drucker, Ernest M., "The Impact of Mass Incarceration on Public Health in Black Communities," **2003**, pp. 151–168.

Lanier, James R., "The Harmful Impact of the Criminal Justice System and War on Drugs on the African-American Family," 2003, pp. 169–179.

Diversity

Bell, Derrick, "The Elusive Quest for Racial Justice: The Chronicle of the Constitutional Contradiction," **1991**, pp. 9–23.

Cobbs, Price M., "Critical Perspectives on the Psychology of Race," **1988**, pp. 61–70.

Cobbs, Price M., "Valuing Diversity: The Myth and the Challenge," **1989**, pp. 151–159.

Darity, William Jr., "History, Discrimination and Racial Inequality," **1999**, pp. 153–166.

Watson, Bernard C., "The Demographic Revolution: Diversity in 21st-Century America," **1992**, pp. 31–59.

Drug Trade

Lanier, James R., "The Harmful Impact of the Criminal Justice System and War on Drugs on the African-American Family," **2003**, pp. 169–179.

Economics

Alexis, Marcus and Geraldine R. Henderson, "The Economic Base of African-American Communities: A Study of Consumption Patterns," **1994**, pp. 51–82.

Bradford, William, "Black Family Wealth in the United States," **2000**, pp. 103-145.

————, "Money Matters: Lending Discrimination in African-American Communities," **1993**, pp. 109–134.

Burbridge, Lynn C., "Toward Economic Self-Sufficiency: Independence Without Poverty," **1993**, pp. 71–90.

Edwards, Harry, "Playoffs and Payoffs: The African-American Athlete as an Institutional Resource," **1994**, pp. 85–111.

Henderson, Lenneal J., "Blacks, Budgets, and Taxes: Assessing the Impact of Budget Deficit Reduction and Tax Reform on Blacks," **1987**, pp. 75–95.

————,"Budget and Tax Strategy: Implications for Blacks," **1990**, pp. 53–71.

————,"Public Investment for Public Good: Needs, Benefits, and Financing Options," **1992**, pp. 213–229.

Jeffries, John M., and Richard L. Schaffer, "Changes in the Labor Economy and Labor Market State of Black Americans," **1996**, pp. 12-77.

Malveaux, Julianne M., "The Parity Imperative: Civil Rights, Economic Justice, and the New American Dilemma," **1992**, pp. 281–303.

Myers, Jr., Samuel L., "African-American Economic Well-Being During the Boom and Bust," **2004**, pp. 53–80.

National Urban League Research Staff, "African Americans in Profile: Selected Demographic, Social and Economic Data," **1992**, pp. 309–325.

————, "The Economic Status of African Americans During the Reagan-Bush Era: Withered Opportunities, Limited Outcomes, and Uncertain Outlook," **1993**, pp. 135–200.

———, "The Economic Status of African Americans: Limited Ownership and Persistent Inequality," **1992**, pp. 61–117.

———, "The Economic Status of African Americans: 'Permanent' Poverty and Inequality," **1991**, pp. 25–75.

———, "Economic Status of Black Americans During the 1980s: A Decade of Limited Progress," **1990**, pp. 25–52.

———, "Economic Status of Black Americans," **1989**, pp. 9–39.

———, "Economic Status of Black 1987," **1988**, pp. 129–152.

———, "Economic Status of Blacks 1986," **1987**, pp. 49–73.

Tidwell, Billy J., "Economic Costs of American Racism," **1991**, pp. 219–232.

Watkins, Celeste, "The Socio-Economic Divide Among Black Americans Under 35," **2001**, pp. 67-85.

Webb, Michael B., "Programs for Progress and Empowerment: The Urban League's National Education Initiative," **1993**, pp. 203-216.

Education

Allen, Walter R., "The Struggle Continues: Race, Equity and Affirmative Action in U.S. Higher Education," **2001**, pp. 87-100.

Bailey, Deirdre, "School Choice: The Option of Success," **2001**, pp. 101-114.

Bradford, William D., "Dollars for Deeds: Prospects and Prescriptions for African-American Financial Institutions," **1994**, pp. 31–50.

Comer, James P., Norris Haynes, and Muriel Hamilton-Leel, "School Power: A Model for Improving Black Student Achievement," **1990**, pp. 225–238.

Dilworth, Mary E. "Historically Black Colleges and Universities: Taking Care of Home," **1994**, pp. 127–151.

Edelman, Marian Wright, "Black Children In America," **1989**, pp. 63–76.

Freeman, Dr. Kimberly Edelin, "African-American Men and Women in Higher Education: 'Filling the Glass' in the New Millennium," **2000**, pp. 61–90.

Gordon, Edmund W., "The State of Education in Black America," **2004**, pp. 97–113.

Guinier, Prof. Lani, "Confirmative Action in a Multiracial Democracy," **2000**, pp. 333–364.

McBay, Shirley M. "The Condition of African American Education: Changes and Challenges," **1992**, pp. 141–156.

McKenzie, Floretta Dukes with Patricia Evans, "Education Strategies for the 90s," **1991**, pp. 95–109.

Robinson, Sharon P., "Taking Charge: An Approach to Making the Educational Problems of Blacks Comprehensible and Manageable," **1987**, pp. 31–47.

Rose, Dr. Stephanie Bell, "African-American High Achievers: Developing Talented Leaders," **2000**, pp. 41–60.

Ross, Ronald O., "Gaps, Traps and Lies: African-American Students and Test Scores," **2004**, pp. 157–161.

Sudarkasa, Niara, "Black Enrollment in Higher Education: The Unfulfilled Promise of Equality," **1988**, pp. 7–22.

Watson, Bernard C., with Fasaha M. Traylor, "Tomorrow's Teachers: Who Will They Be, What Will They Know?" **1988**, pp. 23–37.

Willie, Charles V., "The Future of School Desegregation," **1987**, pp. 37–47.

Wilson, Reginald, "Black Higher Education: Crisis and Promise," **198**9, pp. 121–135.

Wirschem, David, "Community Mobilization for Education in Rochester, New York: A Case Study," **1991**, pp. 243-248.

Emerging Ideas

Huggins, Sheryl, "The Rules of the Game," **2001**, pp. 65-66.

Employment

Anderson, Bernard E., "African Americans in the Labor Force,: **2002**, pp. 51-67

Darity, William M., Jr., and Samuel L.Myers, Jr., "Racial Earnings Inequality into the 21stCentury," **1992**, pp. 119–139.

Hammond, Theresa A., "African Americans in White-Collar Professions," **2002**, pp. 109–121

Thomas, R. Roosevelt, Jr., "Managing Employee Diversity: An Assessment," **1991**, pp. 145–154.

Tidwell, Billy, J., "Parity Progress and Prospects: Racial Inequalities in Economic Well-being," **2000**, pp. 287–316.

Tidwell, Billy J., "African Americans and the 21st-Century Labor Market: Improving the Fit," **1993**, pp. 35–57.

———, "The Unemployment Experience of African Americans: Some Important Correlates and Consequences," **1990**, pp. 213–223.

———, "A Profile of the Black Unemployed," **1987**, pp. 223–237.

Equality

Raines, Franklin D. "What Equality Would Look Life: Reflections on the Past, Present and Future, **2002**, pp. 13-27.

Equality Index

The National Urban League Equality Index, **2004**, pp. 15-34.

Families

Battle, Juan, Cathy J. Cohen, Angelique Harris, and Beth E. Richie, "We Are Family: Embracing Our Lesbian, Gay, Bisexual, and Transgender (LGBT) Family Members," **2003**, pp. 93-106.

Billingsley, Andrew, "Black Families in a Changing Society," **1987**, pp. 97–111.

———, "Understanding African-American Family Diversity," **1990**, pp. 85–108.

Cox, Kenya L. Covington, "The Childcare Imbalance: Impact on Working Opportunities for Poor Mothers," **2003**, pp. 197-224d.

Drucker, Ernest M., "The Impact of Mass Incarceration on Public Health in Black Communities," **2003**, pp. 151-168.

Hill, Robert B., "Critical Issues for Black Families by the Year 2000," **1989**, pp. 41–61.

Hill, Robert B., "The Strengths of Black Families' Revisited," **2003**, pp. 107-149.

Rawlston, Vanessa A., "The Impact of Social Security on Child Poverty," **2000**, pp. 317–331.

Scott, Kimberly A., "A Case Study: African-American Girls and Their Families," **2003**, pp. 181-195.

Stafford, Walter, Angela Dews, Melissa Mendez, and Diana Salas, "Race, Gender and Welfare Reform: The Need for Targeted Support," **2003**, pp. 41-92.

Stockard (Jr.), Russell L. and M. Belinda Tucker, "Young African-American Men and Women: Separate Paths?," **2001**, pp. 143-159.

Teele, James E., "E. Franklin Frazier: The Man and His Intellectual Legacy," **2003**, pp. 29-40

Thompson, Dr. Linda S. and Georgene Butler, "The Role of the Black Family in Promoting Healthy Child Development," **2000**, pp. 227–241.

West, Carolyn M., "Feminism is a Black Thing"?: Feminist Contribution to Black Family Life, **2003**, pp. 13-27.

Willie, Charles V. "The Black Family: Striving Toward Freedom," **1988**, pp. 71–80.

From the President's Desk

Morial, Marc H., "The State of Black America: The Complexity of Black Progress," **2004**, pp. 11-14.

Health

Christmas, June Jackson, "The Health of African Americans: Progress Toward Healthy People **2000**," 1996, pp. 95–126.

Leffall, LaSalle D., Jr., "Health Status of Black Americans," **1990**, pp. 121–142.

McAlpine, Robert, "Toward Development of a National Drug Control Strategy," **1991**, pp. 233–241.

Nobles, Wade W., and Lawford L. Goddard, "Drugs in the African-American Community: A Clear and Present Danger," and **1989**, pp. 161–181.

Primm, Beny J., "AIDS: A Special Report," **1987**, pp. 159–166.

———, "Drug Use: Special Implications for Black America," **1987**, pp. 145–158.

Williams, David R., "Health and the Quality of Life Among African Americans," **2004**, pp. 115-138.

Housing

Calmore, John O., "To Make Wrong Right: The Necessary and Proper Aspirations of Fair Housing," **1989**, pp. 77–109.

Clay, Phillip, "Housing Opportunity: A Dream Deferred," **1990**, pp. 73–84.

James, Angela , "Black Homeownership: Housing and Black Americans Under 35," **2001**, pp. 115-129.

Leigh, Wilhelmina A., "U.S. Housing Policy in 1996: The Outlook for Black Americans," **1996**, pp. 188–218.

Military Affairs

Butler, John Sibley, "African Americans and the American Military," **2002**, pp. 93-107

Music

Brown, David W., "Their Characteristic Music: Thoughts on Rap Music and Hip-Hop Culture," **2001**, pp. 189-201

Bynoe, Yvonne, "The Roots of Rap Music and Hip-Hop Culture: One Perspective," **2001**, pp. 175-187.

Op-Ed

Archer, Dennis W., "Security Must Never Trump Liberty," **2004**, pp. 139-142.

Covington, Kenya L., "The Transformation of the Welfare Caseload," **2004**, pp. 149-152.

Emerson, Melinda F., "Five Things You Must Have to Run a Successful Business," **2004**, pp. 153-156.

Lanier, James R., "The Empowerment Movement and the Black Male," **2004**, pp. 143-148.

Ross, Ronald O., "Gaps, Traps and Lies: African-American Students and Test Scores," **2004**, pp. 157-161.

Overview

Morial, Marc H., "Black America's Family Matters," **2003**, pp.9-12.

Price, Hugh B., "Still Worth Fighting For: America After 9/11," **2002**, pp. 9-11

Politics

Coleman, Henry A., "Interagency and Intergovernmental Coordination: New

Demands for Domestic Policy Initiatives," **1992**, pp. 249–263.

Hamilton, Charles V., "On Parity and Political Empowerment," **1989**, pp. 111–120.

———, "Promoting Priorities: African-American Political Influence in the 1990s," **1993**, pp. 59–69.

Henderson, Lenneal J., "Budgets, Taxes, and Politics: Options for the African-American Community," **1991**, pp. 77–93.

Holden, Matthew, Jr., "The Rewards of Daring and the Ambiguity of Power: Perspectives on the Wilder Election of 1989," **1990**, pp. 109–120.

Kilson, Martin L., "African Americans and American Politics 2002: The Maturation Phase," **2002**, pp. 147-180

McHenry, Donald F., "A Changing World Order: Implications for Black America," **1991**, pp. 155–163.

Persons, Georgia A., "Blacks in State and Local Government: Progress and Constraints," **1987**, pp. 167–192.

Pinderhughes, Dianne M., "Power and Progress: African-American Politics in the New Era of Diversity," **1992**, pp. 265–280.

———, "Civil Rights and the Future of the American Presidency," **1988**, pp. 39–60.

Price, Hugh B., "Black America's Challenge: The Re-construction of Black Civil Society," **2001**, pp. 13-18.

Tidwell, Billy J., "Serving the National Interest: A Marshall Plan for America," **1992**, pp. 11–30.

Williams, Eddie N., "The Evolution of Black Political Power", **2000**, pp. 91–102.

Religion

Lincoln, C. Eric, "Knowing the Black Church: What It Is and Why," **1989**, pp. 137–149.

Richardson, W. Franklyn, "Mission to Mandate: Self-Development through the Black Church," **1994**, pp. 113–126.

Smith, Dr. Drew, "The Evolving Political Priorities of African-American Churches: An Empirical View," **2000**, pp. 171–197.

Taylor, Mark V.C., "Young Adults and Religion," **2001**, pp. 161-174.

Sexual Identity

Battle, Juan, Cathy J. Cohen, Angelique Harris, and Beth E. Richie, "We Are Family: Embracing Our Lesbian, Gay, Bisexual, and Transgender (LGBT) Family Members," **2003**, pp. 93-106.

Sociology

Teele, James E., "E. Franklin Frazier: The Man and His Intellectual Legacy," **2003**, pp. 29-40.

Surveys

The National Urban League Survey, **2004,** pp. 35-51.

Stafford, Walter S., "The National Urban League Survey: Black America's Under-35 Generation," **2001**, pp. 19-63.

Stafford, Walter S., "The New York Urban League Survey: Black New York—On Edge, But Optimistic," **2001**, pp. 203-219.

Technology

Dreyfuss, Joel, "Black Americans and the Internet: The Technological Imperative," **2001**, pp. 131-141.

Wilson Ernest J., III, "Technological Convergence, Media Ownership and Content Diversity," **2000**, pp. 147–170.

Urban Affairs

Allen, Antonine, and Leland Ware, "The Socio-Economic Divide: Hypersegregation, Fragmentation and Disparities Within the African-American Community," **2002**, pp. 69-92

Bates, Timothy, "The Paradox of Urban Poverty," **1996**, pp. 144–163.

Bell, Carl C., with Esther J. Jenkins,"Preventing Black Homicide," **1990**, pp. 143–155.

Bryant Solomon, Barbara, "Social Welfare Reform," **1987**, pp. 113–127.

Brown, Lee P., "Crime in the Black Community," **1988**, pp. 95–113.

Bullard, Robert D. "Urban Infrastructure: Social, Environmental, and Health Risks to African Americans," **1992**, pp.183–196.

Chambers, Julius L., "The Law and Black Americans: Retreat from Civil Rights," **1987**, pp. 15–30.

———, "Black Americans and the Courts: Has the Clock Been Turned Back Permanently?" **1990**, pp. 9–24.

Edelin, Ramona H., "Toward an African-American Agenda: An Inward Look," **1990**, pp. 173–183.

Fair, T. Willard, "Coordinated Community Empowerment: Experiences of the Urban League of Greater Miami," **1993**, pp. 217–233.

Gray, Sandra T., "Public-Private Partnerships: Prospects for America...Promise for African Americans," **1992**, pp. 231–247.

Harris, David, " 'Driving While Black' and Other African-American Crimes: The Continuing Relevance of Race to American Criminal Justice," **2000**, pp. 259–285.

Henderson, Lenneal J., "African Americans in the Urban Milieu: Conditions, Trends, and Development Needs," **1994**, pp. 11–29.

Hill, Robert B., "Urban Redevelopment: Developing Effective Targeting Strategies," **1992**, pp. 197–211.

Jones, Dionne J., with Greg Harrison of the National Urban League Research Department, "Fast Facts: Comparative Views of African-American Status and Progress," **1994**, pp. 213–236.

Jones, Shirley J., "Silent Suffering: The Plight of Rural Black America," **1994**, pp.171–188.

Massey, Walter E. "Science, Technology, and Human Resources: Preparing for the 21ˢᵗ Century," **1992**, pp. 157–169.

Mendez, Jr. Garry A., "Crime Is Not a Part of Our Black Heritage: A Theoretical Essay," **1988**, pp. 211–216.

Miller, Warren F., Jr., "Developing Untapped Talent: A National Call for African-American Technologists," **1991**, pp. 111–127.

Murray, Sylvester, "Clear and Present Danger: The Decay of America's Physical Infrastructure," **1992**, pp. 171–182.

Pemberton, Gayle, "It's the Thing That Counts, Or Reflections on the Legacy of W.E.B. Du Bois," **1991**, pp. 129–143.

Pinderhughes, Dianne M., "The Case of African-Americans in the Persian Gulf: The Intersection of American Foreign and Military Policy with Domestic Employment Policy in the United States," **1991**, pp. 165–186.

Robinson, Gene S. "Television Advertising and Its Impact on Black America," **1990**, pp. 157–171.

Sawyers, Dr. Andrew and Dr. Lenneal Henderson, "Race, Space and Justice: Cities and Growth in the 21ˢᵗ Century," **2000**, pp. 243–258.

Schneider, Alvin J., "Blacks in the Military: The Victory and the Challenge," **1988**, pp. 115–128.

Stafford, Walter, Angela Dews, Melissa Mendez, and Diana Salas, "Race, Gender and Welfare Reform: The Need for Targeted Support," **2003**, pp. 41–92.

Stewart, James B., "Developing Black and Latino Survival Strategies: The Future of Urban Areas," **1996**, pp. 164–187.

Stone, Christopher E., "Crime and Justice in Black America," **1996**, pp. 78–94.

Tidwell, Billy J., with Monica B. Kuumba, Dionne J. Jones, and Betty C. Watson, "Fast Facts: African Americans in the 1990s," **1993**, pp. 243–265.

Wallace-Benjamin, Joan, "Organizing African-American Self-Development: The Role of Community-Based Organizations," **1994**, pp. 189–205.

Walters, Ronald, "Serving the People: African-American Leadership and the Challenge of Empowerment," **1994**, pp. 153–170.

Ware, Leland, and Antoine Allen, "The Socio-Economic Divide: Hypersegregation, Fragmentation and Disparities Within the African-American Community," **2002**, pp. 69–92

Welfare

Bergeron, Suzanne, and William E. Spriggs, "Welfare Reform and Black America," **2002**, pp. 29-50.

Covington, Kenya L., "The Transformation of the Welfare Caseload," **2004**, pp. 149-152.

Spriggs, William E., and Suzanne Bergeron, "Welfare Reform and Black America," **2002**, pp. 29-50.

Stafford, Walter, Angela Dews, Melissa Mendez, and Diana Salas, "Race, Gender and Welfare Reform: The Need for Targeted Support," **2003**, pp. 41-92.

Women's Issues

Stafford, Walter, Angela Dews, Melissa Mendez, and Diana Salas, "Race, Gender and Welfare Reform: The Need for Targeted Support," **2003**, pp. 41-92.

West, Carolyn M., "Feminism is a Black Thing"?: Feminist Contribution to Black Family Life, **2003**, pp. 13-27.

 *appendix III*

ABOUT THE AUTHORS

DENNIS W. ARCHER is President of the American Bar Association and a former two-term mayor of Detroit, Michigan.

KENYA L. COVINGTON is Resident Scholar in the National Urban League's Institute for Opportunity and Equality office in Washington, D.C. She holds master degrees in sociology/criminology, urban planning and a Ph.D. in public policy, University of Maryland, Baltimore County.

MELINDA F. EMERSON is the President of Quintessence Entertainment, Inc. and is the recipient of numerous business awards including the 2002 Woman of Distinction and the Black Business Pioneer. She is also a trustee of the National Urban League.

EDMUND W. GORDON is the Richard March Hoe Professor of Psychology and Education, Emeritus Teachers College at Columbia University; John M. Musser Professor of Psychology, Emeritus at Yale University; and Senior Scholar in Residence at the College Board.

JAMES R. LANIER is Senior Resident Scholar for Community Justice Programs at the National Urban League's Institute for Opportunity and Equality. He holds a Doctor of Philosophy degree in social psychology from the Catholic University of America.

MARC H. MORIAL is President and Chief Executive Officer of the National Urban League and former two-term mayor of New Orleans, Louisiana.

SAMUEL L. MYERS, JR. is the Roy Wilkins Professor of Human Relations and Social Justice at the Hubert H. Humphrey Institute of Public Affairs, University of Minnesota. He received his Ph.D. in economics from MIT and his undergraduate degree from Morgan State University.

CHARLES J. OGLETREE, JR. is the Jesse Climenko Professor of Law at Harvard Law School and Vice Dean of the Clinical Program. This article is excerpted from Professor Ogletree's recently published book on *Brown vs. Board of Education* entitled *All Deliberate Speed: Reflections on the First Half Century of Brown v. Board of Education* (W. W. Norton & Co. 2004).

RONALD O. ROSS is the Dr. Israel Tribble, Jr. Distinguished Fellow for Urban Education Reform at the National Urban League. For more than three decades, Mr. Ross was a teacher and principal in the public schools of New York City and Hempstead, Long Island. He came to the Urban League from his post as Superintendent of the Mount Vernon City School District in New York.

DAVID R. WILLIAMS is Senior Research Scientist for the Institute for Social Research, and Harold R. Cruse Professor of Sociology for the University of Michigan.

NATIONAL URBAN LEAGUE AFFILIATES

AKRON, OHIO
Akron Community Service
  Center and Urban League

ALEXANDRIA, VIRGINIA
Northern Virginia Urban League

ALTON, ILLINOIS
Madison County Urban League

ANDERSON, INDIANA
Urban League of
  Madison County, Inc.

ATLANTA, GEORGIA
Atlanta Urban League

ASBURY PARK, NEW JERSEY
Monmouth County
  Urban League

AURORA, ILLINOIS
Quad County Urban League

AUSTIN, TEXAS
Austin Area Urban League

BALTIMORE, MARYLAND
Greater Baltimore
  Urban League

BATTLE CREEK, MICHIGAN
Southwestern Michigan
  Urban League

BINGHAMTON, NEW YORK
Broome County Urban League

BIRMINGHAM, ALABAMA
Birmingham Urban League

BOSTON, MASSACHUSETTS
Urban League of
  Eastern Massachusetts

BUFFALO, NEW YORK
Buffalo Urban League

CANTON, OHIO
Canton Urban League, Inc.

CHAMPAIGN, ILLINOIS
Urban League of
  Champaign County

**CHARLESTON,
SOUTH CAROLINA**
Trident Urban League

**CHARLOTTE,
NORTH CAROLINA**
Urban League of
  Central Carolinas, Inc.

CHATTANOOGA, TENNESSEE
Urban League of
  Greater Chattanooga, Inc.

CHICAGO, ILLINOIS
Chicago Urban League

CINCINNATI, OHIO
Urban League of
  Greater Cincinnati

CLEVELAND, OHIO
Urban League of
  Greater Cleveland

**COLORADO SPRINGS,
COLORADO**
Urban League of
  Pikes Peak Region

COLUMBIA, SOUTH CAROLINA
Columbia Urban League

COLUMBUS, GEORGIA
Urban League of
  Greater Columbus, Inc.

COLUMBUS, OHIO
Columbus Urban League

DALLAS, TEXAS
Urban League of Greater Dallas
and North Central Texas

DAYTON, OHIO
Dayton Urban League

DENVER, COLORADO
Urban League of
Metropolitan Denver

DETROIT, MICHIGAN
Detroit Urban League

ELIZABETH, NEW JERSEY
Urban League of Union County

ELYRIA, OHIO
Lorain County Urban League

ENGLEWOOD, NEW JERSEY
Urban League for Bergen County

FARRELL, PENNSYLVANIA
Urban League of Shenango Valley

FLINT. MICHIGAN
Urban League of Flint

FORT LAUDERDALE, FLORIDA
Urban League of Broward County

FORT WAYNE, INDIANA
Fort Wayne Urban League

GARY, INDIANA
Urban League of
Northwest Indiana, Inc.

GRAND RAPIDS, MICHIGAN
Grand Rapids Urban League

**GREENVILLE,
SOUTH CAROLINA**
The Urban League of the Upstate

HARTFORD, CONNECTICUT
Urban League of Greater Hartford

HOUSTON, TEXAS
Houston Area Urban League

INDIANAPOLIS, INDIANA
Indianapolis Urban League

JACKSON, MISSISSIPPI
Urban League of Greater Jackson

JACKSONVILLE, FLORIDA
Jacksonville Urban League

JERSEY CITY, NEW JERSEY
Urban League of Hudson County

KANSAS CITY, MISSOURI
Urban League of Kansas City

KNOXVILLE, TENNESSEE
Knoxville Area Urban League

LANCASTER, PENNSYLVANIA
Urban League of
Lancaster County

LANSING, MICHIGAN
Greater Lansing Urban League, Inc.

LEXINGTON, KENTUCKY
Urban League of Lexington-
Fayette County

LONG ISLAND, NEW YORK
Urban League of Long Island

LOS ANGELES, CALIFORNIA
Los Angeles Urban League

LOUISVILLE, KENTUCKY
Louisville Urban League

MADISON, WISCONSIN
Urban League of Greater Madison

MASSILLON, OHIO
Massillon Urban League, Inc.

MEMPHIS, TENNESSEE
Memphis Urban League

MIAMI, FLORIDA
Urban League of Greater Miami

MILWAUKEE, WISCONSIN
Milwaukee Urban League

MINNEAPOLIS, MINNESOTA
Minneapolis Urban League

MORRISTOWN, NEW JERSEY
Morris County Urban League

MUSKEGON, MICHIGAN
Urban League of
  Greater Muskegon

NASHVILLE, TENNESSEE
Urban League of
  Middle Tennessee

NEW ORLEANS, LOUISIANA
Urban League of
  Greater New Orleans

NEW YORK, NEW YORK
New York Urban League

NEWARK, NEW JERSEY
Urban League of Essex County

NORFOLK, VIRGINIA
Urban League of Hampton Roads

OKLAHOMA CITY, OKLAHOMA
Urban League of Oklahoma City

OMAHA, NEBRASKA
Urban League of Nebraska

ORLANDO, FLORIDA
Metropolitan Orlando
  Urban League

PEORIA, ILLINOIS
Tri-County Urban League

PHILADELPHIA, PENNSYLVANIA
Urban League of Philadelphia

PHOENIX, ARIZONA
Phoenix Urban League

PITTSBURGH, PENNSYLVANIA
Urban League of Pittsburgh

PORTLAND, OREGON
Urban League of Portland

PROVIDENCE, RHODE ISLAND
Urban League of Rhode Island

RACINE, WISCONSIN
Urban League of
  Racine & Kenosha,Inc.

RALEIGH, NORTH CAROLINA
Triangle Urban League

RICHMOND, VIRGINIA
Urban League of
  Greater Richmond, Inc.

ROCHESTER, NEW YORK
Urban League of Rochester

SACRAMENTO, CALIFORNIA
Sacramento Urban League